BROOKLYN TO BUENOS AIRES

TRAVELLING DOWN THE SPINE OF THE AMERICAS

Getting to Know the Americas by Wheelchair

Mike Fox

Gotham Books

30 N Gould St.
Ste. 20820, Sheridan, WY 82801

Phone: 1 (307) 464-7800

© 2023 *Mike Fox*. All rights reserved.
No part of this book may be reproduced, stored in a retrieval system, or transmitted by any means without the written permission of the author.

Published by Gotham Books (December 1, 2023)

ISBN: 979-8-88775-491-8 (P)
ISBN: 979-8-88775-492-5 (E)

Because of the dynamic nature of the Internet, any web addresses or links contained in this book may have changed since publication and may no longer be valid.

The views expressed in this work are solely those of the author and do not necessarily reflect the views of the publisher, and the publisher hereby disclaims any responsibility for them.

TABLE OF CONTENTS

Introduction i

Tuesday 1 October 2019
We make it to London Heathrow 1

Wednesday 2 October
Crossing the Atlantic 6

Thursday 3 October
A Pleasant Surprise 9

Friday 4 October
Wall Street and The Jersey Boys 14

Saturday 5 October
The Statue of Liberty and The High Line 18

Sunday 6 October
Worshipping in Brooklyn and Lunching in Queens 24

Monday 7 October
Philadelphia by Amtrak 30

Tuesday 8 October
A Day in the Life of a Mission Community 34

Wednesday 9 October
The Liberty Bell and Independence Hall 37

Thursday 10 October
We make it to Bogotá via Toronto 42

Friday 11 October
Downtown Bogotá 46

Saturday 12 October
Cable Cars and Urban Evangelism 51

Sunday 13 October
Worship, Colombian Style 58

Monday 14 October
Cartagena: A Holiday within a Holiday 66

Tuesday 15 October
Visiting the Old City 70

Wednesday 16 October
Cartagena Beach and our Flight Back to Bogotá 75

Thursday 17 October
On the road to Melgar 81

Friday 18 October
Colombia's Disappearing Railway Map and other matters 87

Saturday 20 October
The Zoo and the Water Park 91

Sunday 21 October
The Best Laid Plans… 94

Monday 22 October
Flying over the Amazon Rainforest 99

Tuesday 23 October
Exploring Buenos Aires 102

Wednesday 23 October
Travelling to Northern Argentina 116

Thursday 24 October
Exploring Salta 122

Friday 25 October
The Trek to Tartagal 127

Saturday 26 October
Exploring Tartagal 132

Sunday 27 October
Delving into the Gran Chaco 136

Monday 28 October
The Journey back to Salta 143

Tuesday 20 October
Excursions in Buenos Aires 147

Wednesday 30 October
Farewell to Latin America 153

Thursday 31 October
A Long Homecoming 155

OTHER BOOKS BY MIKE FOX

Travelling by Road, Rail, Sea, Air (and Wheelchair) in North America

Vamos a Brasil! Recollections of a Volunteer attempting to teach English in Brazil

The Pivo Tour of Slovakia: Memoirs of an Anglo-Slovak student exchange – The Observations of an Outsider

The Italian Therapy Job: A travel Diary

The Wheelchair goes East – Hong Kong, Macau and Mainland China

INTRODUCTION

Our visit to the Americas developed into a travelling experience which grew beyond all recognition from what we originally had in mind. It was only ever meant to be a brief holiday, a relatively short trip to New York, primarily to see and hear the world-famous Brooklyn Tabernacle Choir, which is one of my wife Sylvia's favourite choirs of all time.

I agreed to take her, partly because I really fancied seeing New York, and also so we could visit good friends both in New York and another good friend just down the road (or in our case, railway) in Philadelphia. Well, one thing led to another. A young couple from Colombia, who spent a year in the UK working just a stone's throw, and whom we got to know as good friends, invited us out to see them in their home country. And then, another couple from Argentina, whom we met up with at a reunion in the UK in the summer of 2019, said to us "Well if you're travelling as far as Colombia, it's only a short hop to Argentina!" We couldn't resist. So, a fortnight's holiday transmogrified itself into a full month 'on the road'.

This turned out to be quite a challenge for my wife Sylvia, who has Parkinson's disease and who needs a wheelchair for travelling most of the time, but she was up for it.

Apart from making and re-establishing friendships and my wife's fortitude, another theme which runs through the book is freedom; this latter theme cropped up again and again during our travels. We saw the Statue of Liberty in New York; and we immersed ourselves in the American War of Independence whilst we were in Philadelphia and walked (metaphorically and perhaps even physically) in the footsteps of George Washington.

In Latin America, the two larger-than-life liberators from Spanish colonial rule in the early nineteenth century, Simon Bolivar, and José de San Martin, continue to wield an influence and presence that still seems to permeate life in both Colombia and Argentina respectively; you never seem to be a long way from a statue, square, park or street named after one of these two amazing characters, who liberated half a continent between them. We even visited José de San Martin's mausoleum in Buenos Aires.

As well as meeting old friends and making new ones, I was very much taken by the respect for freedom that comes across strongly in all three nations that we visited, something that perhaps we take a little for granted on occasions back in the Old World.

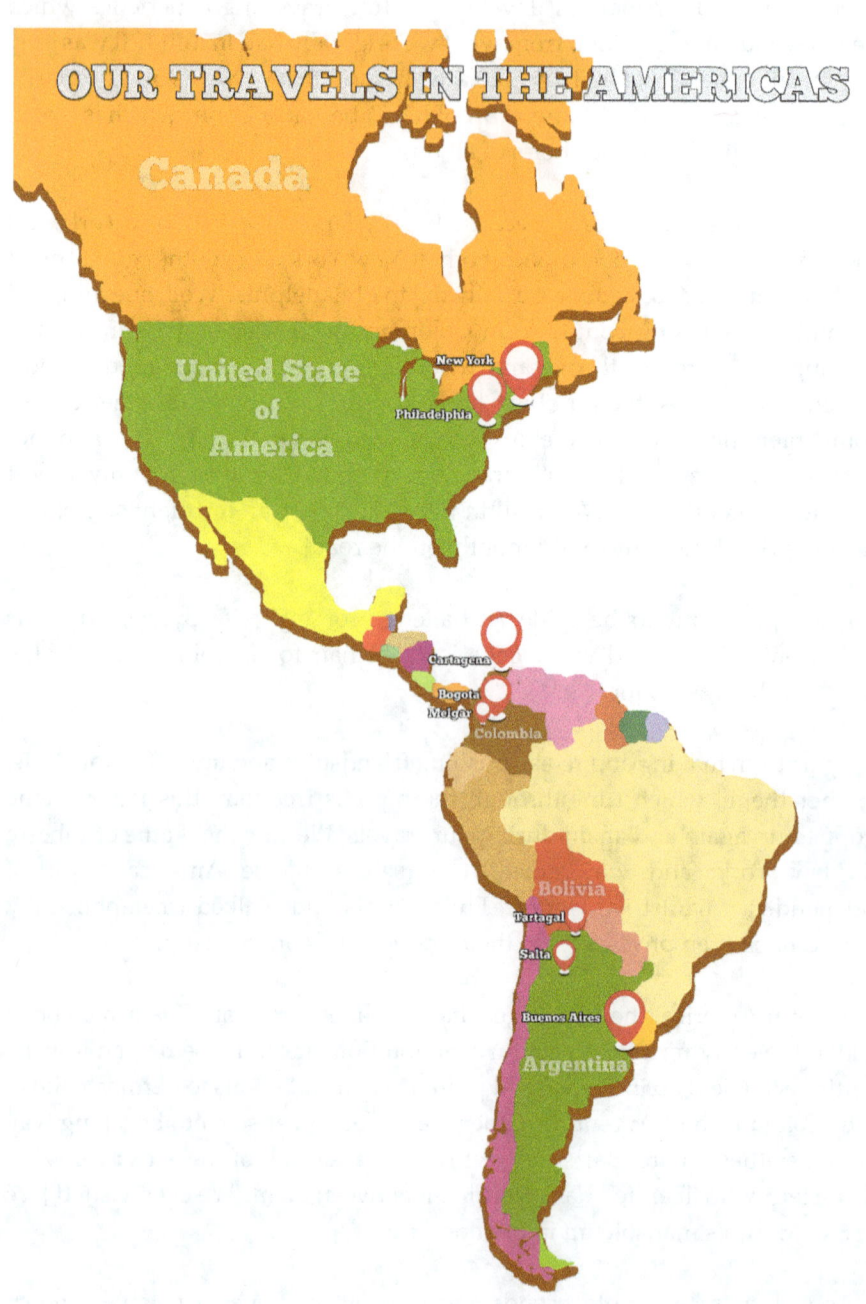

Tuesday 1 October 2019
We make it to London Heathrow

The day starts off with a spot of panic buying; at the last minute I arrive at the conclusion (which I should have tumbled to ages ago) that my travel case to take most of my stuff around the Americas is unsuitable (it's basically too small), and so I drive to our local Marks and Spencer's (M&S) store and buy a new one. I find a case with quite a bit of money knocked off on account of a small dent, but I'm taking the view that it's going to get knocked around anyway in the baggage handling process over the next few thousand miles, so what's the problem with an initial dent? Even the M&S sales lady can't identify exactly where the blemish is!

Downtown New York

Our Italian taxi driver from our home to the station breaks the ice, saying that we will be out of the EU by the time we return in a month's time – "and then the Germans will be in charge" he says. Methinks, he has a point.

There's a delay at the railway station as the disabled ramp is temporarily lost, but our intrepid disabled access attendant eventually retrieves it and disaster is averted; Sylvia is finally able to board the London-bound express train (with me, of course).

The train turns out to be less of an express and more of a stopper – a 'semi-fast' train in the language of the railway books I used to read as a young teenager. In some of the smaller stations where we stop, some of the carriages extend beyond the end of the platform and the train announcer states that people wishing to alight need to make their way through a few of the carriages in order to do so safely. I manage to spill my complimentary coffee by the time we stop at Dawlish, which isn't brilliant, even by my standards. Later on, we are served sandwiches, fruit cake and coffee, all on the house.

Wind and driving rain are followed by more sunshine as we journey through the attractive, pastoral countryside in our almost deserted carriage. Later in the journey, there are still delightful copses which have survived the pressure for development as our train slows down and trundles through the outskirts of Reading, which has transformed itself into a major office centre with a newly expanded station to match. The scheme has given the station more platforms and a plethora of overhead wires, as a consequence of the Great Western Railway electrification scheme.

There is more rain, including a cloudburst as the train passes through Southall and Old Oak Common. The green, copper roof of a Hindu temple glistens in the rain.

Disability help is at hand as we alight at London's Paddington station. We transfer trains to the Heathrow Express for the last leg of our rail journey within minutes. We then encounter a new travel experience at Heathrow Airport; at the Terminal 5 information desk, we are advised to take the 'pod' to our hotel. Our pod is the size of a bubble car, and we just about squeeze our baggage and wheelchair plus ourselves into the limited space available. The pod runs along a guided route, running on an air cushion, along similar principles to the maglev lines, and as far as I know, it could be a maglev design. But the fun comes at a price - £5 per person, in each direction.

After 5 minutes or so, the pod stops and we make our way through a car park to The Thistle Hotel, an anonymous looking two-storey structure with no facilities for the disabled, although it is well related to Terminal 5. Even the restaurant on the first floor is accessible only by stairs. Is this place exempt from the Disability Discrimination Act, I wonder? Our thoughtful travel agent has booked us on the ground floor, but our room is cramped.

There is no manoeuvring space to wheel Sylvia into the bathroom and TV of course no walk-in shower. Getting Sylvia into the one easy chair in the room requires something of the skills of a speleologist, and the whole place has a Stalag feel about it. "It's for one night", Sylvia tells me – "Be positive!" But there's not enough room to swing a dormouse, let alone a cat. Disabled people, keep away from this hotel! A cleaning woman barges into the room, which we have forgotten to lock. I ask if I can help, but she can't understand my English and quickly retreats.

The toilet flush requires the force of an operative of yesteryear working the manual levers in a railway signal box. The television screen is huge, but there again, I have often observed an inverse relationship in hotels between overall quality and TV screen size.

As there is no lift to the dining room, we settle for ordering an evening meal to eat in the ground floor lounge. We sit in close proximity to three larger-than-life ladies, one of whom tells the others how wonderful are people who come from Essex, so no guesses as to where she is from, then.

It is early to bed, ready for an early start in the morning.

Sylvia in the rain, South Manhattan

Empire State Building, New York

Times Square, New York

Broadway, New York

Wednesday 2 October
Crossing the Atlantic

I wake up early and I'm in the shower by six-thirty. It's a nightmare getting Sylvia ready for the day in a place so disabled-unfriendly. Instead of Thistle Hotel, this place should be renamed Thorn Hotel.

Sylvia can't make it up to the restaurant floor with its great view of Terminal 5 and the aircraft taking off and landing. But the restaurant staff are very helpful and one of them carries a tray full of our breakfasts down to the ground floor lounge. And the sun is shining; it's a beautiful autumnal morning, and I can hear the music of Coldplay in the background. At last, I am starting to get a 'feel good' feeling. The breakfast is OK and the coffee tastes good.

We take the pod back to Terminal 5. It's a great system, and in my view, it beats monorail for versatility and fun. As I check in, the official smiles and says: "Your case is 24.3 kilos, but we'll call it 23"; this is just fine with me. In the wheelchair assistance area, we encounter a chatty couple from Texas, Robert and Ronda, whose opening comment is: "What are you guys thinking about over Brexit?" It's probably better not to start an argument. I tell Robert he looks like Ashley Young, a prominent English footballer; he immediately searches on Google, and he seems pleased at the comparison. Ronda, who is very touchy-feely, takes down my mobile number and e-mail. "You will hear from us", she says. (Maybe because I think she likes the sound of Devon.)

We experience a long wait in the security area. It's a good job we are with the access staff, or I would be panicking by now, with less than 30 minutes to go to take-off. As we wait, an English lady next to us says she is off to Tokyo as a lead speaker at a braiding conference; apparently, it's a Japanese form of art, but some Japanese folk saw her in action at a convention and asked her to come over to Japan and demonstrate her techniques, which, I gather, are a British variant on the traditional Japanese way. And quite an honour, I guess.

After the hanging around at security, the pace picks up and a small group of us with pushers race along a passage and then into a lift, before moving quickly to gate B38. Our wheelchair pusher is running at this stage, and I do my best to keep up, with the minutes ticking away. We enter the plane 10 minutes after the scheduled take-off, at around 11:30 am. This is followed by more drama as Sylvia says she has lost her handbag. Fortunately, the stewards have it; how or why they have it is not immediately clear to me, but at least this latest crisis is averted.

We discover that we are not the last passengers to make it on board the British Airways flight to JFK Airport, New York, and we eventually take off at 11:50 for the seven-hour flight. We have a great view of the port wing of the aircraft.

After a couple of hours, Sylvia asks me: "What can you see below?" Seeing as we are crossing the Atlantic, I guess it's got to be the sea. Our air hostess has a Basque name, and she says she comes from a village near Bilbao by the name or Guernica, made famous by Picasso's picture showing the carnage in a village being bombed during the Spanish Civil War – and for Picasso's reply when the Fascist soldiers, looking at the painting, asked him: "Did you do this?", and Picasso's reply was: "No, you did".

Our plane touches down at JFK about 20 minutes late, probably due to our security hold-up at Heathrow. Our taxi, in its famous yellow livery, takes an hour, from three to four o'clock in the afternoon in heavy traffic, to make the relatively short distance from the airport to our hotel in central Manhattan. We travel at almost walking pace in snarling traffic, even on the JFK Beltway. The taxi's radio announces that the temperature is 31 degrees Celsius, officially the hottest 2 October in New York on record. It is uncomfortably hot in the taxi. Our Indian driver, who is very conversational, says the New York rush hour lasts until around 11pm.

The Manhattan skyline comes into view through the heat haze. The Empire State building, which holds its own among the more recent skyscrapers, is clearly a class act of charismatic design. Some of the iconic bridges across the East River can also be seen. This is definitely a bit of a 'wow' factor. But we don't cross on any of the bridges; instead, we take the Mid-Town Tunnel into Manhattan, where the atmosphere changes, and you can almost imagine streets of gold running between the ultra-high rise structures which form much of the character of what is downtown New York.

Our hotel, the Mela, is situated a stone's throw from Times Square, which is perhaps the unofficial city centre of New York, in what appears to be an oasis of calm in this energetic and bustling city. Our hotel room is spacious, in fact no comparison to the nightmare squeeze box we endured last night.

In the early evening, Sylvia and I venture out for a meal. We don't go too far as it is raining; in fact, we settle for a bistro next door to the hotel. Although it is six o'clock local time, our body clocks are telling us it is 11pm. The food is good – lamb-based pasta. Our waiter – I am calling him Fabrice – says that he has lived in France and claims to speak the language. The young waitresses seem to have a great relationship with him, exemplified by lots of laughter and the occasional slap on his shoulder.

Once back in our hotel, it doesn't take long to get to sleep.

Wall Street, Manhattan

Thursday 3 October
A Pleasant Surprise

The five-hour time difference kicks in with Sylvia's medication routine. In fact, she takes most of her tablets at around two in the morning (i.e., 07:00 hrs UK time). But she sensibly delays the water tablets until around eight o'clock local time. Their effect can be devastating, as I discovered taking them for the first time when I was stuck in a traffic jam on the edge of Exeter, with not a public toilet to be had for miles.

As part of our hotel deal, we have tickets for breakfast at the bistro next door. Fabrice is on duty again, with another young waitress telling him he's wrong about something and laughing. One of the waitresses, Deborah, is from Northern Ireland, and has lived over here for 12 years. The problem with Northern Ireland, she says, is that it's full of Northern Irish people, and she says she feels more freedom over here. I try to put in a good word for the people from Northern Ireland, whom I have always got on well with, but I don't think she's convinced.

Paulina, Hector, Sylvia, and Mike on Broadway

It looks set to rain all day and the temperature has plummeted from yesterday's high to a low of 13 degrees Celsius. But time is short to do our sightseeing in New York, and we have tickets for one of the tour buses which can be boarded a couple of blocks away from the hotel. A guy called Sumare, from the Ivory Coast, is directing tourists to the right buses, and he directs us to a bus on the Blue Route, which we catch; Sylvia makes it with difficulty, but her determination wins out.

Before long, our tour bus passes the magnificent façade of Grand Central Station, looking more like a Greek Temple, with its four subterranean storeys of tracks, accommodating 50 platforms (to a railway nerd like me, that figure is impressive); we are informed that there is an exciting new underground rail project, to connect the city centre with Long Island to the east, and it sounds a little like the ambitious east-to-west Crossrail scheme in London. We pass the Chrysler Building, which for a period of five months was the tallest building in the world until it was overtaken by the Empire State Building, which held the record for many years.

World Financial Center, New York

St Patrick's Cathedral, up front, looks like a large building, but it is dominated by its high-rise neighbours. It's still raining. We are driven along Maddison Avenue, the base of one of the bogus publishing companies I briefly teamed up with. Certainly, their New York address was bogus when a friend of mine did some sleuthing on my behalf. I notice that many of the famous yellow taxis in Manhattan carry large billboards on their roofs, advertising films, shows, mobile phones, Amazon prime, fashion accessories, etc - the list goes on. It hasn't caught on in London yet, as far as I know.

We are passing through an area of very expensive real estate; retail stores are guarded by armed doormen (I can see no doorwomen), to ensure there is no plundering from this wealthy part of Manhattan. Central Park appears through gaps in the trees to our left; some 840 landscaped and undulating acres, an oasis of green in high density, downtown New York. Facing towards the park is the Temple Immanuel, New York's largest synagogue.

On the corner of West 50th Street and Seventh Avenue, we alight from the bus and make our way to a great delicatessen, one of several in New York which are admired the world over. And it's easy to see why. They seem to offer a unique mix of delicious and healthy food. We come out of the deli, refreshed after our meal and a rest, back onto the street, ready to engage with another tour bus, covered by our two-day bus passes.

It's still raining as we board our next bus, but I decide to brave the elements and climb up the stairs onto the open top deck. As the bus goes down a hill, one of my shoes is drenched by the surge of surface water gushing to the front of the bus where I am sitting. Unsurprisingly, I am the lone occupant of the upper deck. We pass a small park, known as Bryant Park, a pleasant mix of trees, plants, flowers, and also a ping pong table.

The bus is now going southwards through Manhattan, and briefly to our left we catch a superb view of the approach to the world-famous Brooklyn Bridge, but the opportunity passes for a photograph before I can get my camera out.

Sylvia and I leave the bus at Battery Park, at the southern end of Manhattan. Across the waters of the Hudson River, we can just make out the ghostly outline of the Statue of Liberty through the rain and the mist. This really is not good weather for sightseeing!

It's late in the afternoon and time to return to our hotel. We flag down a taxi, and the driver tells us he is from Afghanistan; he's been over here for 36 years and he's now a US citizen. His kids are getting good grades and there's no way he is going to be returning to his native country. And who can blame him?

Shortly after we return to our hotel room, there's a knock on the door. A waiter delivers a silver tray filled with cheese, biscuits, fruit, gateaux, and wine. We think there must have been some mistake, as we never ordered this. I send them back and then make my way to the brasserie kitchen, where I am informed that the gift has come from a lady named Paulina; she is one of our former students who stayed with us in the UK over a decade ago and whom we will be meeting up with in a couple of days' time. In fact, she aims to see us tomorrow night, as I speak to her on my mobile and thank her for such a pleasant surprise.

There is absolutely no incentive to leave the hotel this evening in search of food; Paulina's treat fits the bill, and we enjoy a lazy evening away from the rain.

Brooklyn Bridge

Steam in the Streets of Manhattan

Mike and Sylvia on the Hudson River, near the Statue of Liberty

Friday 4 October
Wall Street and the Jersey Boys

The morning brings clearer weather, but it's still on the cool side. The New York Times, which I pick up in the hotel, devotes part of its front page to a row over whether 14th Street in Manhattan should be restricted to just buses, kicking out private cars altogether. It looks like we will be able to see this street from our guided bus tour.

It's breakfast in the bistro again, with modern jazz in the background and a lot of conversation at the tables. Sylvia says she's decided New York is a noisy place. And she also thinks the jazz being played in the bistro is rather repetitive. On reflection, I think she's right (on both counts).

A friendly guy on the next table gets talking to us over breakfast. He runs a concert hall just round the block from the bistro, and it's called The Town Hall. "We play an eclectic mix", he says, "including African music and jazz". This sounds interesting. Apparently, the concert hall started life as an educational venue for newly enfranchised women in the 1920s. He says he spent some time in the UK in the 1970s near Shrewsbury, in the Welsh Marches, but after staying there for four years, he says he was still confused about how to pronounce the name of the town, a problem most British people seem to have also.

Deborah, our waitress from Northern Ireland, tells us the Staten Island ferry is free, and then asks us where we went yesterday.

Today we catch the red bus route on the second and last day of our tickets. But we have to find a differently located boarding point, which takes some time. Our bus again turns towards south Manhattan. In amongst the high-rise concrete and glass office blocks and condominiums, we pass a number of truly elegant buildings, some of them, unfortunately, with very limited settings, so they can't really show themselves off. The Flat Iron Building, dating from 1902, slim and elegant, particularly strikes my eye.

The bus goes through the Wall Street area, which is located in the heart of the city's financial district. We alight and find a Chinese deli, where the Chinese language is spoken loudly, even by New York standards. This is a little piece of Hong Kong, where the food is appetising, but the loos are nauseous, and Sylvia in particular is glad to make her escape.

High Line, Manhattan

The National Court Building displays gravitas with its classical façade. But there are also some impressive slim and shining glass towers, somehow fitting for the world's premier financial centre.

We walk down Wall Street, which has a canyon effect from the classical buildings. It reminds me a little of the Inner Temple, just off the Embankment in London. Both have the ambience of a calm oasis, just a short distance from the hustle and bustle of city life. The backwater feel of Wall Street is reinforced by barriers in place to prevent vehicular access (for most people), and they are in the process of reinforcing them. Looking back (northwards I guess), the canyon effect is punctuated by a church spire, whilst the street opens out towards the East River promenade in the opposite direction.

Wall Street is located along the line of a physical wall, built by the Dutch, to keep alien nations away from Niue Amsterdam before the fortification fell to the British in the seventeenth century and the city was renamed New York.

We walk along the East River waterside until we find Pier 16. The next boat departs at 2:30 this afternoon. We buy tickets, giving us time to find somewhere to eat. This is a lively and trendy seaport area with several pavement cafes. We are now experiencing hot sunshine, and we have witnessed huge variations in the weather in just a couple of days here.

Cobble & Company is a typical trendy café, and we stop for lunch here, just a stone's throw from the river. The hot chillies in our meal take us by surprise, but we enjoy the food, as we soak up the atmosphere. Again, there is a lot of noise, but at least it seems to be happy, perhaps semi-relaxed noise.

The happy atmosphere we are enjoying is quickly followed by a crisis. Somewhere between the restaurant and the pier I have managed to lose our boat tickets. The lady at the pay desk refuses to let us go onto the boat.

And even if I bought a new ticket, she says, I couldn't get on the next boat as it is already fully booked. In desperation, I wander down from the pay desk to the officials organising access onto the boat. These people take pity on us, but then realise that the next two boats are fully booked. However, one of them called Sativa, says something really positive and helpful. She advises me that if we can make it to quay number 83, on the opposite side of Manhattan, on the Hudson River, by 09:40 hrs tomorrow, she will personally ensure that we can go on the trip without paying any more money. We thank her profusely.

At around three o'clock, I walk Sylvia back from Pier 16 on the East River near Brooklyn Bridge towards our hotel, near Times Square. I gradually discover that this is a very long way to walk and push a wheelchair, basically from south to central Manhattan. We make it along Broadway and Fifth Avenue. I start to tire, and we do the last half a mile in a taxi (from 32nd Street). But downtown New York is not too bad for wheelchair users, unlike some places we visit later on in our travels.

This evening, we are going to see a show on Broadway. We have agreed to meet Paulina at an Italian restaurant a couple of blocks from our hotel (Cielo on 49th Street). We arrive there from our hotel in good time. At the entrance to the restaurant, however, we do encounter a big issue for Sylvia's wheelchair. The restaurant is accessible only by steps, and quite steep ones at that. Fortunately, two waiters are willing to carry the wheelchair (and Sylvia) up half a dozen steps and into the dining area, which is full of friendly diners. This manoeuvre takes place just before Paulina arrives. Sylvia is especially excited to learn that Paulina and her husband, Hector, have recently acquired a puppy called Noah. We haven't seen Paulina for a couple of years, and the conversation, unsurprisingly, runs and runs. And the food is good.

Sylvia leaves the restaurant with the assistance of the same waiters, and we make our way to the New World Stage Theatre, in West 50th Street. Paulina's husband, Hector, joins us; it's our first introduction to Hector, and what is so great is that we are all relaxed and getting on really well with each other from the word go.

We enjoy the performance of the Jersey Boys in the modern, purpose-built theatre – light years away from the domestic, almost 'living room' architecture of many of the West End playhouses in London. The story of the rise and fall of the band 'The Four Seasons' is moving and funny in places. Several of the songs are well known, at least to me, but I have until now no idea they were sung by The Four Seasons. The expletives, which are uttered in profusion just after the performance starts, in my view contribute nothing to the plot or dramatic effect of the musical. But the music is great.

There is quite a buzz on the street immediately after we step out from the theatre, and we get chatting to a young lady from Kansas, who happily agrees to take a photograph of the four of us. She says she comes to London for work quite often and likes being there.

At around 11:30, we walk back to our hotel through the crowded, lively and noisy Times Square. There's time for hot drinks in the hotel brasserie. We chat for an hour about many things before Paulina and Hector catch the subway back to their home in Queens, which they say is a lot faster (and cheaper) than using a taxi. Paulina agrees to meet us tomorrow at 11:30 in the morning, at Pier 83 on the Hudson River.

South Manhattan Shoreline

Saturday 5 October
The Statue of Liberty and the High Line

Statue of Liberty

This is a race against time to fit everything in, in what could turn out to be a busy day. We have a quick breakfast in the bistro, to the strains of *Lady in Red* before taking a taxi to Pier 83 on the north-west side of Manhattan. We have arranged to meet up with Sativa, who has a soft spot for us after we lost our tickets yesterday, and who has agreed to get us on to one of the boats for no further payment.

Our water taxi is a relatively small craft, with maybe a dozen people on board. This is in complete contrast to the boats we were denied access to boarding yesterday and clearly for the better as far as we are concerned. Moreover, the weather this morning is clear and quite sunny, which is again a contrast to the mist and rain of yesterday. We feel blessed. There is no access problem to the boat (thank you Sativa). Sylvia and I occupy seats at the front of the boat, looking at a great view through a glass screen. Our guide has quite a sore throat, and Sylvia comes to the rescue and offers him a Fisherman's Friend, a powerful cough sweet. The guy is really impressed, and thanks her profusely; Sylvia is his new best friend.

We sail down the Hudson River, with Manhattan on our left and the US State of New Jersey on our right. Although New Jersey has buildings, it is a lot less intensively developed than New York. The word 'suburban' comes to mind, if not quite rural.

Our guide informs us that in 1609, an English explorer, by the name of Hudson, managed to get lost here (which way to London, please?), and the river was named after him. Further downstream, we sail past, on the Manhattan side, a massive urban renewal scheme, which transformed a huge railway layout, called the Hudson Yard, into a multi storey urban project, to the tune of 25 billion US dollars.

At the southern end of Manhattan, there is a new Freedom Tower with a lot of glass, reaching a height of 1,776 ft, housing condos varying in price from 2 million dollars to 52 million dollars; this is an impressive slice of real estate. The Twin Towers are now gone, but our guide, with a fair degree of emotion in his voice, says the city will never be enslaved to terrorism.

We turn up the East River, and dock at a jetty by the name of Dunbow, in the Bronx, on the opposite side of the water from Manhattan. A few people alight from our small ferry, and we catch a great view of the world-famous Brooklyn Bridge, with the angulated Manhattan Bridge further upstream. There is something iconic about the Brooklyn Bridge, which may be linked with the contrast between the stone pillars and supports and the steel superstructure. As our boat rests by the Dunbow jetty, the Brooklyn Bridge rises and falls with the pronounced swell of the East River, resulting in a mixture of euphoria and queasiness.

We also stop on the Manhattan side, near Wall Street, where we tried to catch the ferry yesterday, and a few passengers disembark. There are very few passengers remaining on board as we set off towards the Statue of Liberty, standing on a small island, or rocky outcrop, between Manhattan and the open sea. The huge but elegant Green Goddess looks out over New York and would have been one of the first impressions of the city – and of the United States of America – as people arrived by sea from the Old World. It was a gift from the people of France after the United States won its independence from Britain, probably to wind us up, me thinks.

Approaching the Statue of Liberty, our skipper turns off the boat's engines, and we float close to the beautiful, towering structure. The peaceful atmosphere is a welcome counterbalance to the noisy hustle and bustle of downtown New York, and it's like the world stands still, for a few precious minutes. The guide invites Sylvia and I out onto the foredeck for a closer look at the statue and we pose for a couple of photographs; I think one of them will do for our family Christmas letter.

Our guide explains that the tragic events of 9/11 have resulted in a significant regeneration effect. The destruction of the World Trade Centre moved businesses out of South Manhattan, both to the Bronx, to the south of the East River, and also to New Jersey, on the opposite side of the Hudson River from Manhattan; a secondary cluster of tall buildings now constitutes the New Jersey World Trade Centre.

Finally, we head back up the Hudson River and disembark at Pier 83, with the huge aircraft carrier 'Intrepid' open to the public as a floating museum nearby. Here, we are due to meet our friend and ex-student lodger Paulina in a few minutes, but we (and particularly Sylvia) are distracted all of a sudden by a dog procession. Literally hundreds of dogs pass us on the promenade, with their owners/handlers wearing "Trust your mutt" T-shirts. The 'march past' takes at least ten minutes and it's impressive. Apparently one of the key messages of this canine event is outreach to pets in need. Paulina told us last night that she now has a dog, but where is it?

But one dog does make a beeline for Sylvia, completely out of the blue; it's a terrier, which jumps onto Sylvia's lap as she sits in her wheelchair. The dog's owner, from Upstate New York, says his dog never makes friends with strangers and admits to being very surprised at its affection for Sylvia. I for one am not surprised; it happens everywhere.

Immediately after the dog parade, Paulina shows up a few minutes late (delays on the subway, she says), minus her dog, but it's good to see her. Paulina offers to take us to walk/wheel on the High Line, which in my estimation is one of the most amazing things about New York. Fortunately, we are close to the northern end of this magnificent project. The High Line is a former railway viaduct, running up the west side of Manhattan for close on two miles. Until the 1960s, the elevated railway was part of the New York Central Railroad, and it was used by freight trains. But the rail traffic declined, the line was abandoned, and sections were demolished.

The good news is that the abandoned, derelict line was 'repurposed' as a linear urban park in 2006, and bits have been added to it and continue to be added. At the northern entrance to the High Line, we walk up a ramp which is just about OK for wheelchair pushing. Soon we are looking down onto

Another view of the High Line, Manhattan

around 30 rail tracks at ninety degrees, each one full of rolling stock for passenger trains. I think these tracks run into Penn Central Station, the main station in New York for long distance trains.

Next to the tracks is the Hudson Yards 25 billion dollars redevelopment scheme, one of the most ambitious mixed commercial/residential schemes anywhere in the world. Perhaps the most iconic part of the redevelopment is a futuristic structure called the Vessel, which immediately arrests the eye. Posters by the High Line walkway show photographs of former diesel hauled freight trains which used to trundle along this section, together with pictures of the restoration of the once derelict line, with so much vegetation and even trees, which have taken root. There is a section of preserved rail track in case anyone needs a reminder of what the High Line used to be.

The profusion of landscaping along the elevated walkway is impressive, almost overwhelming. In fact, the High Line has become a victim of its own popularity. The footfall is now so intense that it's almost impossible in places to stop and take photographs without causing human congestion. But it's easy to see why it has become so successful. The views across Manhattan from the elevated route open up new vistas, especially at former rail bridges, for example where the Hudson River comes into sight. But also, the High Line offers close-up views into very expensive real estate, including a futuristic, curved block of apartments designed by the internationally famous architect Zaha Hadid with incredibly long curtains. But being overlooked by the crowds on the High Line may not enhance their saleability at certain levels, where there are excellent views to be had into kitchens, dining and living rooms, and even bedrooms.

In parts, the High Line cuts through overbridges and there are even retail outlets at one point. If a railway has to close, then what better course of action than to create an attractive, landscaped, and imaginative treatment of this elevated walkway, which adds an extra dimension to seeing a lot more of Manhattan than you can do at street level. The route is wheelchair friendly throughout, with several lifts to transport you back to ground level. And this is what we do, taking an elevator down to Chelsea Village, where we make our way to a crowded but friendly restaurant known as Cookshop at the junction of 10th Avenue and 20th Street, in an area known as the Meatpacker District.

As we order our food at around 2pm, Paulina is talking to the waitress and telling her that she is with her parents, who are from England – and initially, I am thinking "no, your parents are from Russia" – and then I realise that Paulina is actually talking about us! Stupid boy! (But nice, though.)

We take a taxi to one of the main bookshops in New York (Barnes and Noble) and buy a map of the city. Paulina then says a temporary goodbye to us and takes the subway home; we walk back to our hotel, which is only five minutes' away, and Sylvia decides to stay in and rest for the remainder of the afternoon.

At just gone 5pm, I start out from the hotel and walk up the Avenue of the Americas to Central Park. I stroll around the park for half an hour or so, although the energy consumed during the day is starting to catch up with me. The park is quite hilly, which takes me by surprise. It even has several rocky outcrops, and a scattering of lakes or large ponds. Central Park is also well covered by trees. Traditional lamps, in the style of the old gas lamps seen on Victorian streets back home in the UK can be seen throughout the park. Facing the southern boundary of the park, a pencil-thin skyscraper is under construction. The park at this early evening hour is full of runners, cyclists and even horse drawn carriages.

I walk back to the hotel in the rush hour. The pavements are crowded, and it takes more time to cross the busy streets full of traffic, and it takes me considerably longer to make the return trip to the hotel on foot.

Central Park, New York

Another view of Central Park

Sunday 6 October
Worshipping in Brooklyn and lunching in Queens

Brooklyn Tabernacle Choir

It's been a difficult night with little sleep, especially for Sylvia. But this is the day Sylvia has been looking forward to for a long time – a visit to the Brooklyn Tabernacle and in particular, its choir.

A taxi picks us up from our hotel for the short journey to the tabernacle, which has three services on a Sunday morning. Our driver comes from the Dominican Republic, and his sat nav gives him instructions in Spanish. We cross over the East River on the Brooklyn Bridge and drive through a mixed (in character, development, and ethnicity) but relaxed area, at least on the surface, and it is a Sunday, of course, when things could be expected to be quieter than during the rest of the week.

As the taxi slows down trying to find the tabernacle, we spot a long queue, snaking round a couple of sides of a block. On seeing this, our driver exclaims: *"Are they are in a line for a church? Are you kidding?!"* He is having difficulties taking it in. He drops us off, and almost immediately a lady beckons to us to follow her, and she directs us to a disabled access point for the tabernacle.

The tabernacle's centre piece is a huge auditorium with tiered seating radiating back from the stage. It reminds me a little of a Victorian music hall. I take a short time out in the little boys' room, and when I return, Sylvia tells me she has been made welcome by an affable lady, who wanted to know where she was from.

By 11 am, when the second service of the day is about to start, there are virtually no empty seats left. A huge information screen tells everyone not to reserve seats for friends, and it then gives the notices of events during the week in English, Spanish, French and Portuguese.

The preacher, going by the name of Ravi Zacharias, preaches a basic, uncluttered, and quite short sermon, but it is the choir, which faces the congregation, that we have really come for. They lead everyone for about four songs, none of which I have heard before, but they are none the worse for that. Sylvia is really enjoying the moment; the principal reason why we have made this trip across the Atlantic.

At one point, everyone is asked to turn and greet a stranger; I get to chat to four Brazilians in the row in front, which is an unexpected pleasure. Like me, they are here on holiday.

We leave the tabernacle and manage to flag down a taxi without too much difficulty. We have a dinner date with our ex-student Paulina and her husband Hector. Our taxi cuts through Brooklyn and into Queens, another of New York's five boroughs. Paulina and Hector live in a 40-storey luxury apartment block, one of three such blocks surrounding a garden, accessible only to the residents of these blocks. These blocks in turn form part of a cluster of modern high-rise flats or condominiums (known as condos), and schemes such as these are transforming former run-down inner-city areas. A similar process is happening in parts of London.

Sylvia's eyes light up when Hector appears in the reception area – or rather (with no disrespect to Hector), when Hector's dog shows up. Noah is a three years old rescue dog with quite a bit of terrier in him. He's friendly enough, and Sylvia is in her element.

Paulina and Hector's apartment block is hyper secure; the lifts are controlled by the concierge on the ground floor. Paulina explains that if, say, you have a friend on the floor below, you can't just take the lift down one floor; you have to travel down to the concierge, who then programmes the lift to go up to your friend's floor!

Another surprise is the number of dogs that reside in this exclusive piece of real estate. And most of them appear to be well behaved. The demographic of the apartments seems to be skewed towards the mid- twenties, with almost no-one coming within a few decades of my age.

We travel up the lift to the pre-arranged floor and we are invited into Hector's and Paulina's apartment. It combines being functional and welcoming, focusing on an attractive, circular dining table. There is an absence of clutter, and I for one, if I were staying here for any length of time, would wreck the pleasant ambience with all my books and work files (and, it must be admitted, my general untidiness).

Sylvia makes friends with a dog in Manhattan

After sitting down to a good meal, we feel a need to walk it off, starting with a tour round the communal garden, before setting off for the best part of a mile down to the banks of the East River, where Long Island faces across to Manhattan. The walkway by the river's edge is maturely landscaped and there is a public park. But the main scenic attraction is the great view over to the high-rise towers in Manhattan, with the yellow girdered Queensborough Bridge a short way off to our right. Commercial traffic plies the river, even today, on a Sunday. Walking along the riverbank, we have stumbled on what appears to be a Hindu wedding ceremony, with beautifully coloured saris and other garments on display.

Paulina points out a recently finished library building, and the entire waterfront area has a community feel about it. A couple of steel gantries standing by the waters' edge are a visible reminder that railway tracks used to be in a place where children now run and play. In addition to commercial shipping, sea planes are landing in the East River and ferries ply back and forth between Queens and Manhattan. There is also a frequent subway service connecting the two boroughs under the water – frequent at least judging by the number of trains rattling over a couple of bridges over the road as we walk back to Hector and Paulina's apartment. Paulina says the subway gets you to Times Square in ten minutes. Some of the subway tracks run over the road on steel viaducts, and one stretch in particular looks straight out of the exciting chase scene in the film *The French Connection*.

Back at the apartment, we enjoy generous helpings of 'key lime' pie, which is Hector's favourite, and China tea. Then it's farewell hugs and promises that Paulina and Hector will come over and visit us next spring. The intention is clearly there, but it remains to be seen whether Hector and Paulina's busy work lives will make this possible.

Our taxi ride back to our hotel takes us over the magnificent steel-clad Queensborough Bridge, where you get the uncanny sensation of driving through a huge cage. Times Square looks as mesmerising as ever, with its scores of moving images and vast crowds spilling out onto the highway.

Once in the hotel, we do the sensible thing and turn in for an early night.

Relaxing in Queens

Manhattan from across the East River

Paulina, Hector, and their dog Noah with Sylvia by the East River

Paulina, Hector and their dog Noah, in their communal garden in Queens

Zaha Hadid architecture, from the High Line

Monday 7 October
Philadelphia by Amtrak

Sylvia has had a good night's sleep and takes her early morning medication on time. But she needs something to eat before getting started. My first task this morning therefore is to go out, walk the streets and find a shop selling cookies. I wander along 44th Street West, which at 07:45 hrs is already busy, being a working day, with lots of passers-by in the streets. Some of the pavement aromas are pungent, and one smell rising from the ground is really obnoxious, maybe linked to the plentiful amount of spilt food on the pavement from the night before.

In between the bars and bistros, I discover a small deli-cum-café and I buy some shortbread biscuits. The Indonesian lady serving me asks whether I have visited her country. When I say I haven't, she replies with "*You will! But don't visit Jakarta – not nice city like New York.*" The lady says that I don't sound English (but doesn't say where she thinks I might be from) before offering me a breakfast for eight US dollars. Later, back in the hotel, Sylvia suggests we go there for lunch.

This is the first time in our holiday that we have to do a total repack of our cases, as today we leave New York and travel to Philadelphia. We start packing immediately after saying goodbye to Jean Marc and his team of waiters in our local breakfast brasserie. Our packing takes an hour and a half and we need to catch a taxi to Penn Central Station as soon as possible; so, no time I'm afraid, to revisit my Indonesian friend and eat one of her lunches.

Penn Central Station, the main Amtrak railway station in New York, is unprepossessing from street level; it doesn't have the Cathedral-like presence of Grand Central. But it has an extensive layout of rail tracks below ground level. We are escorted down to the platform for our train to Philadelphia by disability staff, who are impressively efficient. Every train entering the station is heralded by the atmospheric bell-like sound of a klaxon.

Amtrak 609, our express train to Philadelphia, moves out of the station on time, and immediately we enter the tunnel taking us beneath the Hudson River. A train announcement informs us that no food or drink is being served on the train today, which comes as a bit of a blow as we had held back from eating lunch so far, thinking we could do so on the train.

We emerge from the tunnel into the New Jersey daylight – this is a world apart from New York – a separate US State. Our train passes some industry but mainly open countryside with the Manhattan skyline rising up in the background. Our train crosses several waterways and railway lines on steel bridges.

Our first stop is Newark, New Jersey, in a town which is spread out but lacking much in the way of serious high-rise buildings, with few structures over two or three storeys. The pace, unsurprisingly, appears less frenetic than in New York.

Further on, we pass through a series of affluent looking settlements, probably providing home to commuters working in New York, separated by many acres of woodland. But the trees haven't yet turned into the myriad of colours that are associated with the New England Fall. We encounter a lot of red, white, and blue liveried locomotives charging past us at speed, making my attempts at photographing them challenging.

After about three quarters of an hour into our journey, we come to an unscheduled halt, which we are informed is due to a broken-down train ahead of us. Eventually we get the all-clear after railway staff walk along the side of the track, for what purpose I am unsure, and we start off again. Shortly afterwards, the train trundles into the town of Trenton, where we can see a lot of dereliction and evidence of former heavy industry. It looks like typical 'rust belt' country. We pass buildings covered in graffiti, rusting rail tracks, empty factories, and shells of structures, punctuated at one point by a huge billboard, saying just one word in capitals: HOPE.

We are now approaching the city of Philadelphia, which has an extensive built-up area. The city's downtown skyscrapers appear in the distance. The train slows down, and we stop at the main Amtrak station in the city, known as Thirtieth Street Station. Sylvia and I alight here and change trains quite smoothly, thanks to the excellent support staff, who take us up to the higher level tracks via an elevator. There's just time to spot a long freight train crossing over on a bridge at an even higher level.

Our suburban train takes us out of the station, exactly on time (3:07 hrs in the afternoon) on the final leg of our railway journey to a place by the name of Fort Washington. I glance at a map showing the extensive network of suburban rail lines fanning out from the city centre, a system known as SEPTA – Southeast Pennsylvania Transportation Authority. On this map, I notice that the airport is at the southern end of the network, i.e., at the opposite end of the Philadelphia conurbation to where we are headed; this is bad news, as we need to catch an early morning flight on Thursday morning!

Our mid-afternoon train is almost empty, and Fort Washington station is devoid of any railway staff when we alight. Outside the station there is a huge car park for the commuters making their way into the city each day. But the place is eerily quiet in mid-afternoon, and there is no one to advise on taxis, and no taxis in sight. After a while, a helpful passer-by gives us a phone number to ring for taxis, but the company just tell us to ring back in half an hour. We make contact with a second company, who say they will pick us up in 30 minutes. But after 45 minutes, with no taxi in sight, I ring them again, whereupon they inform me that we are outside their range. Why they couldn't have told us that nearly an hour ago is beyond me.

In desperation I phone the WEC headquarters, where our friend Betty lives and where we will be staying (hopefully) for a few days. I get through to a friendly guy called Dan, and he drives over to the station and picks us up, or should I say rescues us, at 5:30. The waiting has been quite an ordeal for Sylvia, although the weather has been dry and mild, so I guess it could have been a lot worse. The stress of waiting has been compounded by a number of fairly aggressive flying beetles, who are persistent in their 'welcome'. They are also very adept at avoiding being trodden on or swatted. It is good to eventually get away from the station.

Dan drives us to the WEC mission headquarters, focused on what seems like a nineteenth century country house, next to a small stone castle-like structure. It is situated on the aptly named Camp Hill, which occupies the summit of a gentle mound and is surrounded by trees. Philadelphia's urban sprawl seems a long way away from this countryside location. Several accommodation blocks have been added around the original house over the years, but the site retains its pleasant, rural character. Wild deer also roam through the estate.

It's good to see our friend Betty again, whom we first met when we taught English for a few weeks in Brazil, just over a decade ago. She greets us and shows us our room for the next few days. She even has a pot of beef stew on the boil – a welcome sight, even more so seeing as we haven't eaten anything since our breakfast at 08:30 this morning, seemingly light years away if the pangs in my stomach are anything to go by. Considering Betty has had an eye operation today, this stew is no mean achievement. Sylvia is wheeled into the communal dining area, whilst I am left stirring the beef stew.

Sylvia and Betty in Downtown Philadelphia

We are introduced to two of Betty's friends, Marolyn, and Susan, both former career missionaries who worked in the Ivory Coast, and another lady who worked in Italy. They are all concerned that Betty should not overdo things so soon after her cataract operation. We are impressed by the welcoming atmosphere, even though we are in a real sense strangers in this place.

The stew turns out to be excellent, and is eagerly anticipated, especially by me. This is one of my most memorable and enjoyable meals of our entire travels. We are in bed before ten o'clock, and both of us are dog tired.

Tuesday 8 October
A Day in the Life of a Mission Community

I awake to the sound of a klaxon of a freight train at around 05:00 hrs this morning. I remember hearing the sound of freight trains in the small hours of the morning the last time I visited the United States, which I find both haunting and endearing. Why do they appear to be silent for the rest of the day?

After consuming a breakfast of cereals and a bagel, we walk around the extensive mission campus. It is known as Camp Hill, partly because it is a hill (and a pleasant, green one at that) but also because this was the spot where George Washington camped with his troops at a key moment during the American War of Independence. He apparently had around 15,000 troops at the time and from this height they could monitor the movements of the British army which was based in Philadelphia below.

We walk across to the oldest building on the campus, known as the Castle, past a flock of guinea fowl, who apart from adding visual interest, apparently feed off the ticks that come with the deer, which roam around the mission compound and in and out of the surrounding woodland. The guinea fowl certainly seem to spend most of their waking life eating stuff on the ground.

In the Castle we are introduced to some of the team that manage the mission, as well as a pastor who is usually with his church in Morocco. He says that in Morocco, anything overtly signifying a Christian church or fellowship is banned. It's also not a good idea for converts to Christianity to advertise the fact on social media, which can lead to 'consequences'.

Around the middle of the day, one of Betty's friends, Susan, drives us a few miles to a restaurant, or diner, called 'Michael's', which for some reason they deem an appropriate place for us to visit. The chicken salads we order are truly mountainous, and we are given boxes to take home anything we can. Susan drives us back through a hilly area which is mainly rural in appearance, but which is dotted with expensive real estate, reflecting the fact that it is within easy commuting distance of Philadelphia. There is also a lot of woodland, and the area seems well served by churches, a couple of which would not be out of place in the English countryside. One stone-built edifice even boasts a tower which looks like it dates from the Norman Conquest!

Part of the extensive grounds of Camp Washington

The Castle, Camp Washington

After we return to the mission compound, I spend an hour or so walking on my own through the woodland on the edge of the estate; it is easy to find areas of tranquillity where the only sounds are birdsong, although the sound of traffic on an inter-state highway occasionally disturbs the peaceful ambience.

At half past five, we wander over to the main house for the evening meal. The age range of the resident mission family, if that is the correct way to describe it, is from a few months old to nonagenarians, and the atmosphere is convivial and relaxed. We are introduced to people working in several countries, including Spain, The Gambia, Tibet, and the Ivory Coast. Every newcomer is introduced at the meal, and Betty gets to her feet and introduces us as English teachers in Brazil! The Thai green curry is great, but I'm still feeling bloated from the voluminous chicken salad we consumed (or tried to consume) at midday. Everyone at our dining table is welcoming, and this experience has been constant the whole time we have been here.

A deer and two fawns are grazing in the semi-darkness as we leave the dining area at the end of our meal and make our way back to our accommodation. We are located far enough away from the urban area to enjoy dark night skies here.

We return to the main house later in the evening, where Betty has organised a showing of what can loosely be described a musical based on the Old Testament story of Ruth. As a Biblical character she is unusual (although not unique) in being both a Gentile and a hero. The production lasts two hours, and it is really dark when I wheel Sylvia out onto the grounds, past the chattering crickets and back to our quarters.

Once back in our room, we set about doing some of our packing, although our early departure is not scheduled until the day after tomorrow. We are in bed by midnight, after I have read about 50 pages of Sebastian Faulks' *Paris Echo*.

Betty seems to have recovered well after her eye operation yesterday. It's nice how many people on the campus come up to her and ask how she is. We have been privileged to catch a glimpse of what goes on at this amazing place.

Betty's friend Susan, Betty and Sylvia at Fort Washington

Wednesday 9 October
The Liberty Bell and Independence Hall

I pack most of my case just after breakfast, which strikes me as easy and hassle-free, and there seems to be a lot of space left over; in fact, too much, and I am trying to think what I have forgotten to pack for the next leg of our travels to Colombia, which we embark on tomorrow. Initial euphoria gives way to mild concern. I have the rest of the day, however, to figure out what is in danger of being left behind in George Washington territory.

The plan for the day is for us, with our mentor, Betty as our guide, to visit the city of Philadelphia, and in particular its historic associations with the American War of Independence. Betty's close friend, Susan, drives us down to the nearest railway station at Glenside to catch the suburban train to downtown Philadelphia. But after the train stops at the station, the four steps up onto the carriage from the low platform prove too much for Sylvia to manage. Susan by this time has driven away from the station! Clearly, we have to find a station with a disabled access facility, and our 'saviour' Dan, who rescued us two days ago, cheerfully comes to our assistance again and drives us to a disability-friendly station at Fort Washington, where we wait for the next train into the city.

Betty is in a good mood this morning; her eyes are looking a whole lot better than they were yesterday. There are no stitch marks remaining, only two days after her operation. This is excellent progress and really good news.

We alight from the train at Jefferson Station, which is in the heart of the city, around midday. As I give my ticket to the clerk at the barrier, he says: "Keep talking, I love your accent!" There's not really an answer to this (except, perhaps, to stop talking).

In the street, it starts to rain, and we seek refuge in a Starbucks café. A local artist kindly offers us a chair. His pictures are weird, but he is a warm person and easy to chat to.

We drag Betty through a clothing store (I get the impression that Betty is not really into retail therapy) as Sylvia is after a raincoat (but is unsuccessful on this occasion). We then walk along Market Street, one of the main thoroughfares in the city centre, and join a queue to see the original Liberty Bell with its irreparable crack.

It is free to view the Bell, and it's as if it is the birth right of all Americans to make the journey at some time in their lives to this hotbed of American independence.

The Bell is a hugely significant symbol of American liberty and independence. Appropriately, it is tastefully housed within a new purpose-built building, which has plenty of room for information boards, telling us all about the war for American independence, and why the Bell symbolises US freedom from British rule. The crack in the Bell dates back to when it was cast by a British iron foundry, which was granted the commission by the fledgling US government. However, so the story goes, the foundry managed to drop it, hence the crack. You could call it incompetence. In a number of ways, the British do not come out of this story in a particularly good light. It seems to serve the independence story well and the British part in it, to say that the crack is irreparable.

Another part of the extensive grounds of Fort Washington

The Bell is situated with a large plate glass backdrop, enabling it to be viewed from outside in the street across a pleasant green area planted with golden and purple flowers.

Outside in the street, it is still raining as we enter the area of mainly older (some dating back as far as the eighteenth century) buildings known as the National Historic Park. Clusters of traditional buildings are interspersed with parks, and there are statues of revolutionary leaders occupying the focal points. A statue of George Washington faces Independence Hall, which dates from 1713. Its original name was the Pennsylvania State House, and it was the administrative centre of the British colony of Pennsylvania.

We also find Independence Square, which again is punctuated by statues and is surrounded by fine buildings in what is the historic core of Philadeiphia. The biggest challenge is negotiating a satisfactory access for Sylvia's wheelchair; we almost give up but find a way on the 'final' corner entrance to the square, before aiming for the queue awaiting access to Independence Hall. I have to say that I am impressed with Betty's stamina; she is a good few years older than us, and she is walking really well in inclement weather. If anything, I am the one who is struggling to keep up!

We manage to gain inclusion to the next guided tour of Independence Hall, and our larger-than-life guide informs us with his resonant, booming voice that the interior is 90% original. Our guide takes us through the two main rooms – the court and the assembly. One of the highlights is the chair where George Washington, we are informed, sat as he deliberated over meetings of the assembly.

In 1776, Thomas Paine, the revolutionary writer, is credited with influencing public opinion in favour of independence from Britain, and the American War of Independence then spreads to all 13 British colonies in the New World. Initially, there was division about whether to sever ties with the home country, based as much on economic arguments as to ties of kith and kin. But by 1784, it is all over, and the United States of America emerges as an independent, sovereign nation. Our guide tells us that, following a big war between Great Britain and France in the 1760s, although Britain came out on top, the country was broke and it started taxing the American colonists at rates guaranteed to sow discord amongst the locals.

The colonists wrote to the King of England, George III, asking for some respite from the heavy taxes; the king ignored the letter and didn't even give the colonists the dignity of a reply, let alone any reasoning for the tax hike. This burning sense of injustice created fertile ground for the War of Independence. Why did we have such a plonker on the British throne? Apparently, the lack of conviction on the British side is underscored by the fact that two top British generals refused to take command of the British army in America. As the story unfolds, I feel an increased sense of sympathy with the colonists, rather than with the out-of-touch British colonial establishment.

The newer buildings showcasing the Liberty Bell and the Independence Centre fit in well with and are subservient to, the eighteenth-century Independence Hall and don't detract from the urban grain of the historic part of Philadelphia. We wander into the Independence Centre and watch a film featuring the delights of this varied and attractive city.

This is followed by a brisk walk in the light rain back to Jefferson Station, where we catch an express train back to Fort Washington. We are in bed soon after nine in readiness for our early morning flight to Bogotá tomorrow.

Downtown Philadelphia

Historic grounds, Philadelphia

Pennsylvania Courtroom, Philadelphia

Liberty Bell, Philadelphia

Thursday 10 October
We make it to Bogotá via Toronto

Our alarm sounds at 05:00 hrs, shattering a strange dream I was having concerning a well-known barrister riding away on a horse. I clearly need to see a psychiatrist.

By six o'clock, we are in Betty's car which is being driven by Susan, on our way to the airport. It is dark as well as being early, and the highway is busy, verging on serious congestion.

Susan hands me a piece of paper with travel instructions on how to get to the airport, as she is not familiar with the route. It's not the right time to say that I am struggling with her handwriting. Later, Sylvia finds the sat nav on her mobile and it works perfectly, although it is a little strange to hear the voice with an English accent giving us directions on an American highway!

There are final hugs and thankyous at the entrance to Philadelphia Airport Terminal D. We have enjoyed our few days in Philadelphia/Fort Washington. As I am waiting for our flight, I receive a text message from my visa company, informing me that my credit card is about to be terminated, with a new card to be issued to our home address. Mild panic ensues. After several seconds of red mist, I notice that my card has an emergency phone number to call. Fifteen minutes later, after going through the security questions, I am reassured that my existing card will be good to use until 2 November, when I shall be back in the UK. Crisis averted. I now feel a whole lot more awake on this early morning!

Airport security has its quirks. I am asked by the officials if I am 75 or older. When I say "no", I have to take off my shoes as I go through the security machinery. I guess you have to draw the line somewhere, but I think it's the first time I have taken off my shoes on the off-chance that I may be a shoe bomber.

Our first of two flights that we will be catching today takes us to Toronto, where we change to our second flight to Bogotá. Our Toronto-bound flight takes off on time and just before we are enveloped in cloud, the Delaware River comes into view, with its docks, quays, and shipping, including what resembles a warship.

Street market in central Bogotá

Further into the flight, the clouds part and we can see the wooded Appalachian Hills below. This is Upper Pennsylvania, part of the famous Rust Belt. It may be economically depressing on the ground but from up here, the landscape has a verdant, undulating beauty, and most of the industry seems to be screened by the trees. Sylvia meanwhile is making friends with an inquisitive toddler with large blue eyes, looking at us from the row immediately in front; at one point the toddler gives us a high five, which the parents find amusing, as do we. The clouds manage to obliterate Lake Eerie, but we do get glimpses of Lake Ontario before the plane is prepared for landing at Toronto.

We experience a smooth transition at Toronto Airport through to the gate for the Bogotá flight, with a wheelchair pusher called Kouziel (I think) from the Cameroun at the helm, giving Sylvia a pleasant ride between terminals.

The pleasantness continues with a smooth entrance into the Boeing 767 aircraft bound for Bogotá. Sylvia explains her problem with her right knee to one of the stewardesses, who says that she has the same problem which has prematurely kept her out of playing soccer.

It's a clear, bright afternoon as we take off from Toronto and fly over Lake Ontario, which appears like a sea at first, but which then seems to contract to the size of a lake as the far shore comes into view. I spot a river flowing through a series of pronounced meanders in hilly terrain. Could this be the Upper Hudson River, which eventually flows out to sea by the Statue of

Liberty, but this is my imagination working overtime. I can't access a map on the plane to show me where I am flying over, and I haven't a clue about our exact route to Colombia.

Further into our flight, the landscape changes into what looks like a series of grey, barren, scoured ridges with few signs of habitation. Further along, a wide river can be seen. Is this the Mississippi or Missouri?

Eventually, the skies darken, and I sink my head into my latest novel – *Paris Echo*. Sylvia tries to interest me in a card game on her tablet, but it demands far too much intelligence for me to pick up and I retreat back to reading my book. About an hour before landing at Bogotá, the crew ask if there is anyone with medical knowledge on board. After we land on the airport tarmac, several medics and assistants board the plane, and everyone stays seated for about 30 minutes to let the medical team do what they have to do before they take the sick person to hospital. The atmosphere remains calm throughout, which I guess is a tribute to everyone and especially the emergency services.

At the baggage reclaim, we are challenged by an airport official about one of our cases, possibly because I let it go a couple of times on the carousel before I took it off. The reason for my earlier hesitation is that our thick, bright red plastic name and address label has become detached from the case (never to be seen again), and I was using this as my initial point of reference.

After some questioning, the airport official asks for my boarding card, which of course has the tags proving ownership of the cases. However, when we changed flights at Toronto, we were given new boarding cards, and somewhere along the line I have mislaid the original Philadelphia to Toronto boarding cards (I hope everyone is keeping up with this). The official is not impressed, despite the fact that our names are clearly written on a luggage label. At this point another, more pragmatic, official intervenes, offers her opinion, and pronounces that we are free to go.

All the delays mean that our programmed 9:30 pm arrival becomes a 10:30 rendezvous with our friends Gabriel and Natalia, who have waited patiently for us to appear through the arrivals gate. We know this couple from when they worked at a Christian Conference Centre for a year near to our home, and who invited us out to spend some time with them in Colombia. Coming out of the airport, it feels pleasantly cool with a slight wind. This is great for us, although our hosts say they feel chilly!

The next challenge is fitting our entire luggage, plus the wheelchair, into Gabriel and Natalia's average size car, but they rise to the occasion impressively. We leave the airport car park and hit the city streets, which at this late hour are relatively free flowing. Our hotel in Bogotá, the Wyndham, appears at first glance to have all the mod cons, and we have a large, disabled-friendly room. We are in bed just after one in the morning.

View of Bogotá from breakfast room, Wyndham Hotel

Inside Gabriel's family's jeweller's shop, Bogotá

Friday 11 October
Downtown Bogotá

Natalia's parents, Raulfo and Liliena, together with Natalia and Gabriel, at the Wyndham Hotel, Bogotá

Over breakfast, we discover, as we look out over an expansive view of the city surrounded by mountains, that Bogotá sits at about 7,800 ft above sea level. This statistic could explain a lot. Both of us, but especially Sylvia, had a bad night's sleep, primarily caused by breathing difficulties. Sylvia also feels nauseous and at one point says she thinks our room is shaking. I am not quite so convinced about any shaking but the shortage of breath is real enough.

People are very friendly at breakfast, including a South African tourist by the name of Moses. After breakfast we wander down to reception and meet up with our friends Gabriel and Natalia.

We are introduced to Raulfo and Liliena, Natalia's parents, who it transpires, are both Geography teachers, who teach in the same school and who have side-by-side offices. It doesn't get much cosier than that! Apparently, we will be meeting them later in our visit to Colombia when we will travel to their hometown of Melgar, about 100 miles from Bogotá and which sits at a much lower altitude, and where the climate, consequentially, is considerably hotter than here.

Gabriel and Natalia start our tour of downtown Bogotá by taking us down to the jewellery quarter. We enter a rabbit warren of tiny jewellers' shops on several levels within a substantial traditional building. It is a condensed version of the world-famous Hatton Gardens jewellery quarter in London, the scene of a multi-million-pound (sterling) diamond heist, where thieves drilled through internal walls and blew up safes in the small hours, just a few years ago. The Bogotá jewellery district has a friendly and close, neighbourly feel to it. It is clear that many of the jewellers working here are like a big family. The huge amount of money tied up here means that there are armed guards patrolling, which detracts from the ambience of intimacy to an extent.

From the jewellery quarter it is a short walk into the central square in the city – the Plaza Bolivar, named after the liberator of Colombia from colonial Spanish rule in the early nineteenth century. The primary Cathedral of Colombia, dating from 1609, extends along one side of this large square. It is one of several beautiful, colonial style buildings which define this principal meeting point, and none of them look out of place, even though there is some variation in architectural detailing. The National Assembly faces the southern side of the square, and its colonnades remind me of the British Museum.

There is a lot of activity within this extensive plaza. On one side, there is a band playing typical Andean flute music. Two colourful alpacas are being paraded and there are over-friendly pigeons. There are many market stalls selling traditional local products, including some from the Amazonas region to the east of the country. At one of the stalls, Natalia buys some strange looking paste, which she says helps her with pain relief.

Dominating the square stands a larger-than-life statue of the man himself. Simon Bolivar occupies the central place in the square which is named after him. It is clear that the man is still revered in Colombia.

Around lunch time, we return to the jewellery shop and meet Gabriel's parents, Henri, and Leonora, plus his sister, Ingrid, who also works in the shop; it is a complete family venture, and Gabriel is the third-generation jeweller in his family. We are invited to drink a cup of pure Colombian coffee, which seems a bit more special than the coffee I consumed earlier in our hotel.

Ingrid has studied beauty treatment and massage, but she seems to enjoy working here with her close-knit family within this intimate neighbourhood. Ingrid volunteers to massage Sylvia's leg, in the back of the shop, and this is clearly a labour of love. She uses the green 'sludge' that Natalia bought in the main square just half an hour ago. Sylvia enjoys most of the massage. Ingrid puts everything into massaging; she has firm hands, especially for someone so small and slender, but she also has great skill and dexterity, and it is eye opening to see such an artist at work.

Whilst Sylvia is undergoing her massage, a trader comes into the shop with an Italian figurine, with the aim of selling it to Gabriel's father. Gabriel and his mother, Leonora examine it closely with a magnifying glass, and everyone stops chatting. The result is no sale. I'm not completely sure why; maybe some blemish is revealed in the magnified examination, but I have to say the figurine looked great to me with my untrained eyes. It's perhaps a good job that I am not a jeweller!

Gabriel then takes me for a walk around the jewellery quarter. He knows a good half of the people in the neighbouring shops, nearly all of whom appear to be working in family run enterprises like his family's shop. Gabriel takes me into a number of the shops, or workshops, with their crowded work benches. It's amazing they know where anything is, and I am sure if it were me, I would be losing items left, right and centre.

One guy I am introduced to, who is apparently working on his own, is making – or is it crafting – a pure gold bracelet, and he hands me the constituent parts; and then I realise, for the first time in my life, just how heavy pure gold is, which comes as a shock to me. He is working to a commission for the bracelet, and he reckons it will take him a week to complete the task. The work clearly demands creativity, great attention to detail and enormous reserves of patience.

Gabriel takes me into several other jewellery shops, and it becomes clear that many of these dealers in minerals and precious stones specialise in individual niches; some make jewellery and other beautiful artefacts, some sell and some are involved in repair work, and many of them deal in specific materials, such as gold, silver, gem stones, etc. It is also clear that there is a symbiotic relationship between many of these artisans, artists, specialists and retailers, and there is great camaraderie. Several of them hug and embrace Gabriel, and they all seem pleased to see him.

Around two o'clock in the afternoon, Gabriel takes me to a local restaurant and orders traditional Colombian food for us to eat in his parents' shop. The main ingredients are chicken, rice and small, round potatoes and a green sauce, which may sound strange to our British taste buds, but the food is delicious as we consume it in the small back area of the shop. Gabriel shares with us his vision for starting up a jewellery workshop for aspiring would-be next-generation jewellers, and hopefully it will come to pass. Long may this special, intimate, creative area continue to flourish.

After our meal, it's time for another walkabout/wheelchair push, and we visit an art museum which is dedicated to a Colombian artist by the name of Fernando Botero, who painted his pictures in the early twentieth century. The people he created are larger than life, literally. He drew and painted his models as rotund, not just people who could wear plus size clothing, but who are grotesquely chubby and broad about the beam. Exactly for what purpose Botero created these expansive characters, I am not sure; in fact, the whole museum/gallery experience confuses the senses, although I find myself enjoying it in a perverted sort of way.

One of Botero's exhibits is an oversized, almost grotesque Mona Lisa, which I admit amuses rather than repels me. Interestingly, one picture of a naked, full frontal, and of course, fat woman, goes by the title of 'The Letter'. But it cannot be said in all honesty that the letter in question is the first thing you notice about this in-your-face painting. He also has a penchant for big bottoms, not all of which are covered up; he paints plenty of sights for sore eyes!

It's nice to catch some fresh air after the Botero experience, and on a neighbouring street corner we admire the exterior of a beautifully detailed colonial era church, the *Iglesia de la Candelaria*, which took from 1656 to 1703 to construct. Then, in the early evening, as the number of vehicles dies down to a degree in this city famous for its traffic congestion, we manage to find a quiet corner, overlooking some colourful flower beds. Here we order drinks from a local bar and chill out. This exquisite part of the city does not appear to have changed since it was part of the Spanish Latin American Empire.

Fish mural in Bogotá

Downtown Bogotá

Saturday 12 October
Cable Cars and Urban Evangelism

Sylvia, Gabriel and Natalia, central Bogotá

Sylvia and I both manage to catch up on our sleep, which is a huge blessing, although I am far too relaxed first thing in the morning, resulting in our getting down to breakfast too late. As a result, we keep Gabriel and Natalia waiting in the hotel reception for a few minutes. They are very gracious and understanding about it.

Our plan for this morning is to take the cable car up to the edge of the mountainous rim, part of the Andean chain, which defines the eastern side of the city of Bogotá, at a height of 9,500 ft (3,150 metres) above sea level. This is the best part of 2,000 feet above the basin where the city lies. Close to the summit of the cable car, there exists the church of Monserrate, which can be seen from all over the city below as a prominent landmark. How they transported all the materials up to build this impressive and large ecclesiastical edifice all those centuries ago is baffling; maybe mountain goats came into their own?

Sylvia, sitting in her wheelchair, ensures that we get priority boarding onto the cable car, which then progresses smoothly up the mountainside. At the summit, there is an area lined out with the famous Stations of the Cross, depicting scenes from Jesus' sufferings at Calvary, two thousand years ago. The only possible route for wheelchairs is challenging, to put it mildly, but

Gabriel, as always, is up to the task and is happy to take over wheelchair pushing duty to negotiate the difficult bits. I feel it is only gracious to let him

Bogotá Central Business District

do this! The thinness of the air is even more noticeable at this great height, and I struggle for breath on occasions, even when I am walking slowly.

There is a religious service in progress in the church of Monserrate, and we try and enter the building, conscious that we must appear like intruders rather than worshippers; this is not the most appropriate moment to take photographs. The service is packed, with all the seats taken and with continuous standing along the sides. One of the two officiating priests is a musician. He takes to the keyboard with gusto and belts out several catchy, contemporary sounding songs, none of which I am familiar with, but the congregation clearly know them and join in singing enthusiastically. There is quite a lot of written material in the church on the subject of mission, which is clearly close to their hearts, and what little I pick up from the preaching is clear and direct.

We leave the church, and the weather is clear if a little cool at this high altitude. The Andean chain of mountains on the opposite side of the city is clearly visible, although the clouds are coming in lower, the longer we stay and admire the extensive view. Can there be a more beautiful setting for a capital city? Looking down across the city, we can make out key features, such as the Plaza Bolivar and the surrounding traditional buildings, such as the Cathedral and presidential palace. One of the really good things about the planning of this city is that the cluster of the tallest buildings (say, about 12 storeys plus) in Bogotá, is located well away from the historic core of the city and its setting. Gabriel points out the airport runway, which is just about visible far away to our right.

Back in the city centre, 'El Zaguan del Humo' is a friendly gastronomic establishment which serves traditional Colombian food. Within a few minutes of arriving there, we are joined by Gabriel's parents and his sister Ingrid, fresh from a morning's work. Natalia then tests me regarding my openness to Colombian culture by asking me to drink a local concoction by the name of lolla (?). Is this some form of ritualistic initiation? Everyone seems keen to know my view on this drink for some reason. My response – "*It is interesting*" – doesn't cut any ice with any of the onlookers. It is heavily spiced and totally strange to my palette. I don't think this is going to be the last time I will be faced with this drink whilst we are in Colombia.

View of Bogotá from cable car

I have a feeling our sons, Nathan, and David, would fancy visiting this place. We are each served with a different dish, with the aim of everyone sharing everyone else's food. It sounds like a good plan to me. Poor Ingrid gets teased by everyone as she consumes a lot, despite her diminutive figure. But why not – the food in this place is excellent.

Around four o'clock, we leave the centre of the city and drive for about 45 minutes to a barrio (neighbourhood) known as Eden but resembling more of a fallen paradise. We have come to observe and take part in a project which is reaching out to children and young people in the neighbourhood. In an open, flat area defined by high railings in the shadow of several high-rise blocks of flats, which is big enough to accommodate 5-a-side football matches, somewhere in the region of 80 kids are charging around or playing various different games, none of which involve expensive equipment. (We are informed that the number of kids here was double the week before.) Instructions are shouted out via a megaphone, and there is a small group of adults and older teenagers directing activities. Gabriel and Natalia are involved with this project every Saturday afternoon.

It is impossible for Sylvia to gain access to the 'action' unaided; the ground is just too rough. Several older teenagers rise to the challenge and pick up the wheelchair, with Sylvia sitting in it, and carry her over some rough ground from where Gabriel's car is parked and place her within the games area. Within minutes, or even less, she is surrounded by friendly children and teenagers, some wanting to try out their English, and all of them interested in where she is from. Appropriately, even a dog trots up to her, a kind of long haired 'Dulux dog', which stays by her side. I am finding it difficult taking a photograph of her, as she is virtually hidden in all directions by children, all trying to ask her questions.

A smaller number of the kids also chat to me. They want to know where I am from – and my age. I ask them to guess my age, and I am really pleased when several say 50 and then revise it downwards to 40! When I tell them to increase the number, they say 60 and then laugh because they think they are being cheeky. I am enjoying this. What wonderful kids!

After a while, Sylvia and I are introduced by Gabriel and Natalia to the local pastor who spearheads this cutting-edge urban evangelism. His name is Pastor Aldo, and he is known as and looks like a biker. This is not an exaggeration. He is stocky, bald, and wears a biker's jacket and a friendly smile. But it is clear that he has an excellent relationship with the local children and young people, and that he and his team are doing a great work in this needy area.

After the games, the leaders give a short message over the loudspeaker. There are also messages in graffiti on the sides of the housing blocks overlooking the games area. Someone has painted a Christian slogan quite high up on the nearest wall, which reads: *"Neither religion, nor church nor pastors – only grace."* No one seems to know the author of this thoughtful graffiti, or at least the authors are not owning up to it. Interesting.

Gabriel, Sylvia and Natalia near cable car summit, Bogotá

One of the lads, 12-year-old Angel, is wearing a Manchester United T shirt. I clearly have to chat to him and say I that come from Manchester and he happily lets me take a couple of photographs of him.

As it happens every early evening in Colombia, and in fact on every day of the year, which still comes as a surprise to me from the temperate latitudes, it gets dark quickly, at just after six o'clock. Several children and teenagers come over and shake our hands as we prepare to leave. I am particularly impressed at the sight of everyone clearing the site of any litter; I couldn't guarantee this being the case back in the UK.

Gabriel and Natalia take us back to our hotel by around 7pm, and we arrange to meet up in the morning at a quarter past nine to attend a service at Pastor Aldo's church. I wonder whether we will see any of the kids there whom we met today.

Steps of the church of Monserrate

Market in Plaza Bolivar, Bogotá

Site of urban evangelism project in Barrio Eden

Sunday 13 October
Worship, Colombian Style

Bogotá Cathedral

Botero Gallery, Bogotá

We finish our breakfast in the hotel just about on time to meet up with Gabriel and Natalia. They drive us out to the Candelaria district in the south of the huge urban area of Bogotá, home to upwards of seven million souls, for a church service which starts at ten this morning.

Traffic hazards abound in this city, even on a Sunday morning. Apart from frequent random lane changing, usually to gain a few yards in the congested streets, another bit of excitement is that on occasions, some cars in front of you suddenly brake for seemingly no apparent reason or to let somebody out; occasionally, cars also stop in an instant without pulling over, so as to allow someone making their living off the street to wash their windscreens or sell them something (or even polish their shoes). In these traffic conditions, Gabriel has to remain totally alert, and we feel safe with him driving us. But the colourful markets along the main roads add a touch of vibrancy to the street scene, and there is never a dull moment.

Pastor Aldo's church turns out to be his home within what appears to be a quiet, established residential area of terraced housing; it's definitely not rough enough to be classified as a 'barrio bajo' or favela. The pastor himself, looking relaxed and smiling, looks the complete biker as he sits astride his Harley Davidson motorbike, just outside the front door, welcoming everyone coming into his church. We are ushered inside, right up to the front, and people make way for Sylvia's wheelchair to pass easily.

Plaza Bolivar, Bogotá

A large domestic sized room, which possibly is the lounge for the rest of the week, is packed with chairs, and our front row seats face a low stage, upon which a group of musicians are in full swing in the warmup to the service. The music is extremely loud, but nevertheless attractive on the ear, at least, that is, on mine. Almost everyone we can see at the gathering, which comprises maybe fifty to sixty people filling every available square foot of the ground floor, looks like they are below the age of 30. We are therefore conspicuous in our longevity.

The service officially gets underway with enthusiastic singing, and it sounds like everyone is joining in. The pastor is one of the people on the stage – in fact occupying centre stage – microphone in hand, giving it everything. There is no doubting his commitment, passion, and sincerity, and we can easily see why Gabriel and Natalia are attracted to this fellowship and want to throw in their lot with it. There are at least three vocalists in addition to Pastor Aldo on the stage; one female, maybe in her early twenties, has a good, strong voice and two lads of maybe a similar age, also in biker gear, sing their hearts out. There is absolutely no shortage of enthusiasm here.

Also, on stage there is a drummer, two guitarists and a 15-year-old girl on the keyboard, who tells us at the end of the service that she has only been learning the instrument for about a year. She is picking up new techniques and tunes by the week; there is nothing like learning on the job, of course. We sing about three songs at the outset, all with a lively tempo, and none of which I know. The words, in Spanish, of course, come up on a big screen which is situated at the back of the stage, but they are largely obliterated by the on-stage musicians. (This is not a problem for most of the congregation, who probably know the words anyway, or soon will do.)

Some of the teaching is portrayed by messages and pictures on a large screen, and this morning, we are taken on a whistle-stop tour of the book of Exodus in the Old Testament, including the Ten Commandments. This is followed by a recording of the well-known secular song (Carole King, I seem to recall) *'What the world needs now, is love, sweet love'*, which I remember from the pop charts several decades ago, but a song which clearly retains its appeal. After the youngest children leave the main room for their separate teaching, Pastor Aldo preaches for about an hour, using Paul's letter to the Colossians in the New Testament as a springboard. He preaches with passion, reminding us that as Christians, we have a new purpose in life. He stresses the Bible's importance as a 'road map'.

In a departure from the way services are generally conducted back in the UK (or at least in relation to my take of what is 'normal'), coffee is served for some of us, Sylvia and I included, about halfway through the pastor's message. Is this to keep me awake, I wonder? Has someone been talking about me?

Pastor Aldo on his bike, outside his church

Inside the church

At some point, an interpreter (into English) appears on stage, and I am not sure whether this is exclusively for our benefit. We discover at the end of the service that the guy, whose name is Andrés, spent most of his childhood in New York, and this explains the high quality of his English. Another feature, which I would guess happens more rarely in the UK, is the sight of several children making their way into the service as it progresses, and no one bats an eyelid. Some of them were at the event we visited at the kick about area yesterday afternoon and are clearly voting with their feet to get involved and hear more. A more cynical interpretation is that they arrive minutes before drinks and biscuits are made available to everyone.

One of the impressive things about the pastor, apart from his passion, is that he talks for over an hour with no notes. He ends giving us a few challenges – for whom in your life are you making a path? Is your life an expression of God's love? His message has been clear and uncompromising, and you are left in no doubt as to what, or who, he believes in.

Another view of Plaza Bolivar

At one point in the service, Sylvia and I are prayed for as "the brother and sister from Great Britain". It would be tempting to become more involved with this place, like Gabriel and Natalia, were we ever to become residents here.

After the close of the formal service, the musicians are keen for Sylvia to play the keyboard. (Clearly, someone has told them that Sylvia is a musician) They all crowd around her once she is seated at the piano keyboard, and then applaud her rendering of 'The Splendour of the King'.

At the end of the service, I also chat to Andrés the interpreter, about whether the church which is (a) very noisy and (b) lies within an established residential area, has ever been the subject of any complaints from nearby residents. He tells me that one near neighbour complained to the municipality about what he considered were excessive noise levels coming from the church. Apparently, the Council's environmental protection officer came round and asked the complainant: "Is the church making any loud noise before nine o'clock in the morning?" The answer was "no". The officer then asked him whether there was excessive noise after nine at night? Again, the answer was in the negative, at which point the officer told him he didn't think there was a problem…I'm not sure that an environmental health official in the UK would have taken the same view!

After chatting to folk for some time after the close of the service, it's genuinely hard to tear ourselves from these lovely and enthusiastic people, and it is three o'clock before we finally drive away from Pastor Aldo's fellowship (and we are not the last to leave). I hope we can buy some CDs of the songs we have just heard in this service at some future point.

Somewhere near the city centre, we stop for, what is by now, a late lunch at a restaurant in a big shopping mall in a district by the name of 'Ciudad Bolivar' (Bolivar City…it's that man again). We are soon joined by Natalia's mum and dad, and I feel we are beginning to get to know them. After our light meal, I then, with the help of Gabriel, use a cash point and help myself to my first Colombian pesos.

Sylvia at the urban evangelism project, Barrio Eden, Bogotá

Mike with some of the kids from the project

We are back in our hotel by early evening, where we spend time packing for our flight to the seaside town and port of Cartagena tomorrow morning, and spend time organising our laundry requests.

Port of Cartagena

Sylvia at the piano after the service

Monday 14 October
Cartagena: A Holiday within a Holiday

Ingrid, Natalia, Gabriel and Sylvia enjoying a meal at Restaurant El Zaguan del Humo, Bogotá

The alarm is set for six-thirty in the morning, to give us a fighting chance of catching the 07:30 airport bus from the hotel. These early morning schedules are a big challenge for Sylvia (and for me, if I am honest). We make the bus with a few minutes to spare. Traffic in central Bogotá is light, as it's a bank holiday, and we arrive at the airport at 08:00 hrs.

At the airport, there's no sign of Gabriel and Natalia. We feel a slight moment of apprehension, as neither of us can remember whether Gabriel and Natalia have bought the airline tickets – and where are they, anyway? Just then, my mobile pings, and it's Gabriel saying they have our tickets, which they copy onto my phone screen (this is cutting edge technology for me), and then we make contact with them at the boarding gate, to the strains of Tears for Fears' *"Come on, come on, I'm talking to you!"* which seems appropriate at this moment.

On our internal flight to Cartagena, the guy in the next seat to me is very chatty, and the time passes quickly. On the descent into Cartagena, he hands me his card, and says we can contact him anytime. He turns out to be a captain in the Colombian Navy, which he says is modelled very closely on the Royal Navy, even down to its uniform and rankings. Apparently, it all stems back to a British admiral who came over here in the late nineteenth century and basically set up the Colombian national navy. He tells me that this British admiral is regarded as a hero in Colombia. I say to him that I don't think we would be having this conversation in Argentina, which brings a smile to his face.

As we fly over an industrial area on the outskirts of Cartagena, a little girl in the row behind exclaims *"It's dirty!"*, which amuses everyone, especially me. I guess industrial areas are!

We walk out of the airport arrivals area, straight into a noisy and lively street scene, with a lot of touting for taxi services, in a temperature noticeably higher than back in Bogotá. This place really does look and feel as though you are in the tropics.

Our taxi takes us along the Cartagena waterfront facing the Caribbean Sea, past a huge stone wall which defines the historic city, possibly the first landing place of the Spanish conquistadores in the whole of South America. And on to our hotel, which is a 29-storey edifice located on the opposite side of the busy main road which runs alongside the beach.

Our hotel room is expansive, accommodating two double beds with plenty of room to spare. But the first thing I notice is the sea - it's right in your face, as it were, through huge floor-to-ceiling glass windows, and there are semi-distant views towards the old, walled city to the right. This is quite a wow factor from the fifteenth floor.

At around two in the afternoon, the four of us venture out of the hotel in search of a late lunch. Cartagena is certainly beautiful and vibrant, but its pavements are a real challenge for wheelchair access! In fact, we soon come to the conclusion that the only way to successfully push Sylvia towards any restaurants is in the road, where some taxi drivers register their frustration at having to drive round us. But we find an atmospheric restaurant with flamboyantly dressed waitresses and waiters, who serve us in between dancing to the intoxicating beat and sound of music which reminds me of Cuba. The fish we order tastes of being freshly caught, and it is accompanied by local flavours of fruit juice. A beautifully colourful bird even joins us and perches on an adjoining table. Sylvia eats her first substantial meal in days, as she has been suffering from a sore throat.

Just after four o'clock, we cross the busy main road outside the hotel, and Gabriel manages to drag Sylvia in her wheelchair over the sandy beach to within a few metres of the edge of the sea. Sylvia decides she's not going to risk getting any part of her body wet, and she stays and chats with Natalia. Gabriel and I join the noisy throng of swimmers who are enjoying the gently undulating waves, the wonderfully firm sandy base, and the fact that this warm coastline shelves at a very gradual gradient; the warm sea remains shallow – at least for me it's not out of my depth - for maybe up to a couple of hundred metres from the shoreline. These are perfect conditions for a relatively weak swimmer like me to feel safe and comfortable.

Gabriel is clearly quite an experienced swimmer, both on the surface and underwater. In contrast to all his energy, I tend to lie on my back and let the sea do all the work. A few high-speed boats roar past the swimmers without too much of a gap, and it does seem like a kind of free-for-all off the Cartagena coastline.

At six o' clock, the police come and close the beach for public use. Gabriel explains this is for at least two reasons: firstly, the waves are higher, and therefore more dangerous, at night when they respond to the pull of the moon, and secondly, there are no lifeguards on duty at night. But apparently some people just wait until the police have gone and then swim back into the water again!

We are aware of another problem, which has an obvious solution; there are no pedestrian crossings over the main road from the hotels to the beaches. It is even worse for wheelchair access, especially because there are no dropped kerbs on the beach side of the road. In order to enable Sylvia to cross in safety, I stride out further and further into the road, and eventually a car stops. This is followed by impatient car horns from drivers behind the good-mannered guy who stopped for us to cross the road.

Back in our hotel room, we turn off the lights and catch an atmospheric view of the sea in the impending darkness through the huge plate glass windows. I can't recall ever seeing such a full-on view of the sea from a hotel bedroom window.

The four of us eat our evening meal in the hotel restaurant and then sit by the outdoor pool on the second floor which overlooks the bay, with the twinkling lights of the historic city in the distance, off to the right.

Around ten at night, our peace is shattered when, in attempting to close one of the huge floor-to-ceiling curtains in our room, I inadvertently manage to bring the entire curtain rail crashing down on my head. I go down and report it at the reception. By the time I return up to our room, two workmen are just completing fixing it.

The lady manager of the hotel, Dona, informs us that, as from tomorrow, we will be moved to a new room which will have better disabled facilities for Sylvia. Which is great, but the room faces away from the sea and the view isn't as good!

Simon Bolivar statue, Cartagena Old City

Dona, our hotel manager, Hotel Dubai, Cartagena

Tuesday 15 October
Visiting the Old City

Cartagena Old City

Sylvia wakes up feeling unwell, with a swollen throat. Around seven in the morning, she can't take her regular medication for fear of choking. We ring Gabriel and Natalia, who speak to reception. At about the same time, Dona, the manager of the hotel knocks on our door, bringing a disabled toilet with her, and says the hotel has an emergency doctor, who will visit Sylvia soon.

Thankfully, Sylvia is starting to perk up; and there is visible relief all round. Natalia says her mother has a doctor friend who lives just outside Cartagena. I think of the guy on the plane who left me his card. One way or another, I think we are covered. One of the waiters brings up some melon and orange juice for Sylvia, and she successfully takes her medication. I then go down for breakfast with Gabriel, and one of the waiters brings what we have selected on a tray to our room. By nine-thirty, Sylvia is transformed and raring to go.

Dona comes up to our room a few minutes later and tells us the bad news: a lot of damage has been done overnight to the room we were going to move into (not by me, I hasten to add), and it will take several hours to fix. So, in the meantime, she asks, would we mind temporarily using a room on the 27th floor, where Sylvia can take a shower?

We take the lift to the room on the 27th floor with Dona. This room has huge, floor-to-ceiling windows on three sides; I guess it's a bit like a penthouse, or what I think a penthouse might look like, seeing I've never stayed in one. These windows look out on to the city, resort, and port of Cartagena.

A word about the geography of this place; our hotel is situated on a narrow peninsula, just about wide enough to accommodate two parallel roads, running along an east-west axis. This separates the 'pleasure' side of Cartagena, to the north of this narrow strip, where it faces the sea, from the naval and commercial port which operates in and around a huge inlet to the south. There are several cargo and container vessels in the port, whilst alongside the quays nearest to our hotel, a couple of small warships, possibly corvettes, are moored close to each other.

Cartagena Waterfront

Initially, we are informed that we can only stay in this penthouse until the repairs are carried out to our pre-arranged room. But when Dona returns, she says we can stay in this penthouse room tonight; Sylvia has clearly worked her charm on her.

Dona is someone who cares about the impact of the hotel on the guests, and the surrounding area, and is keen to improve things where possible. We share with her our views about the importance of making pedestrian access from the hotel across the busy main road to the beach safer, more convenient, and more disabled friendly. Why not put in place pelican crossings, dropped kerbs and ramps?, we ask. These suggestions would not need to be very expensive, but their health, amenity and even economic benefits would be substantial. It seems a 'no-brainer' to us.

Dona then goes a couple of steps further: "Why not part-pedestrianise the road and limit access to the remaining half of the main road to cyclists and buses?" she says. "And while we are at it, why not segregate a section of beach for private use, for use by some of the hotels?" I guess this would involve having to install gates and patrols. Dona suggests this seemingly draconian course of action because she says the continual pestering of holiday makers by a succession of hawkers, who try to sell items such as beach hats, cigarettes, ice cream and jewellery, every few minutes, needs to be eradicated. She has a point, although I have been to worse places, and in my view, the trade is inevitable everywhere that rich play goers rub shoulders with the poor locals. And it's probably not a bad thing to be made aware of the local population rather than be cocooned off from them.

This interesting discussion is interrupted by the arrival of the hotel doctor at 11:30. Sylvia is prescribed a course of anti-biotics for her developing tonsillitis. The doctor is really friendly and wants to know where we are from, saying he used to live and work in America. Although his name is Guillermo, everyone in his hospital in the States called him Howard, because they were expecting someone by the name of Howard to come and work there! And the name stuck. When he returned to the same hospital, several years later, they all welcomed him back as Howard!

We also get to know a few things about Dona and her life story. She tells us that she is a single mum, with two offspring of whom she is immensely proud. Her son is a naval officer, whilst her daughter travels the world with her work. She says although she is a single mum, she is looking for a boyfriend – and then adds: "Maybe an Englishman!" She also says that she worked in Iceland where she managed a similar hotel to this one; she says she wants to return there, as her bosses here in Cartagena have promised her benefits and then reneged. She says the Icelandic people are very welcoming and they loved the colour of her skin, but she says she doesn't have their beautiful blue eyes. She only returned to Colombia because she was homesick.

Dona also says she is proud to come from Medellin, Colombia's second city. In particular, she is proud of the fact that the city recently constructed a tunnel connecting the airport to the city centre, with no financial assistance from China or anywhere else for that matter. "The Bogotá people are jealous", she says, "they say it was financed through drug money". Competition is clearly alive and well between Colombia's two principal cities.

Just as I am feeling relaxed and ready for the day, Gabriel takes me up to the top floor of the hotel and says "follow me" – across what is termed the crystal walkway. It's a bridge across two parts of the hotel structure, but with a difference; you can see through the floor, which looks like glass, and which gives you a perfect view down to the street below. I have certainly changed to a lighter shade of pale right now.

In the afternoon, we opt for a spell in the hotel swimming pool, where the water is colder than the sea. Sylvia gets changed and we help her into the water, or at least she manages to get her feet wet, as opposed to total immersion. The doctor's anti-biotics tablets apparently only start kicking in tomorrow morning, and right now, she's still feeling under the weather.

We witness a beautiful and rapid sunset over the sea. The setting sun lights up the whole sky, its clarity possibly enhanced by the short rainfall of a couple of hours ago. Many romantic pictures are taken on mobiles by hotel guests in the setting sun, a few of them falling into the risqué category.

A 'flotilla' of five pelicans flies past, seemingly in formation. They are such elegant creatures when flying, showing off their long, graceful necks. The lady selling drinks at the poolside bar asks if I am an English speaker, and when I say yes, she then asks me if I am American. I say I am from 'Inglaterra' (England) and she appears surprised. She says she is trying to learn English to help her with her job and her career prospects in general, but she is finding it really difficult. I write down for her the names of a couple of free language apps that I know of.

After dinner, at around eight o'clock, we set off from our hotel to the old city by taxi. We are dropped off by one of the gates in the substantial city wall, which has certainly been a bastion of defence in times past. In one of the squares, there is a statue of a guy by the name of Pedro de Heredia, who is credited with designing the original city in the sixteenth century. He is one of only a handful of town planners worldwide that I have seen celebrated in this way. Gabriel says that the city is where the Spanish first arrived in Colombia, so it has a huge historical significance for the nation.

The principal square, however, is the Parque del Bolivar, which is dominated by a statue of Simon Bolivar, the liberator on his horse. It is a verdant square, well covered by trees and mature plants, and it is easy to understand why it is called a park rather than a square. The huge main church sits just off the square and at this dark hour it is illuminated by the Torre del Relogio (the Clock Tower). This tower, with its cupola, is the dominant feature of the old city, and it is visible from a long way outside the city walls, including from our hotel.

The old city is laid out in a matrix of narrow streets with rough pavements, even for walkers, and an even rougher challenge for wheelchairs; Sylvia unfortunately gets quite a bumpy ride. There is a strong sensation of the smell of horses, or at least of matters associated with horses. Within these narrow streets there is competition for priority between motorised taxis, horse-drawn carriages, and pedestrians; human traffic has to be on high alert to stay clear of danger. But the volume of traffic slows everything down to manageable levels. The taxis in particular can be quite aggressive, and I spot the warning *"guarda su distancia"* (keep your distance) on the back of one taxicab; I wonder if the *distancia* is measured in inches!

We stop at a café for late night drinks at 10:30 pm, and even at this hour the streets are still lively. My cappuccino feels red hot, and it takes 20 minutes or so to consume it. A group of fair-haired girls in short – and in one case minimal – skirts sit at the next table in the café. Gabriel says they are from Argentina by their accents. However, I totally fail to pick up on any differences in the way they are speaking!

Outside the café in one of the plentiful squares in the old city, we hire a taxi, arriving back at our hotel sometime after eleven o'clock. The four of us agree to meet up for breakfast at 08:30 and we have to check out by 12 noon. We make our way up to bed in our wonderful penthouse suite overlooking the world. We are soon too far gone in our slumbers to appreciate it.

Sylvia in the water

Wednesday 16 October
Cartagena Beach and our flight back to Bogotá

Sunset over Cartagena

At around five-thirty in the morning, early dawn daylight streams in through the windows of our penthouse suite. At six, I take photographs of the sunrise over the Bahia de las Animas. At around 08:15, a container ship makes its way into the harbour. Despite the commercial nature of the port, it has great beauty. Beyond the bay, I can make out a green, rolling landscape.

After breakfast, the four of us head for the beach. Gabriel negotiates a price for beach chairs and a shelter, and then the two of us plunge into the sea for the last time. A couple of hours pass in an instant; it's all too relaxing, and I'm sure the salt water is relaxing my right foot, which has been aching a little in recent days.

Along the beach comes the relentless tide of hawkers that Dona spoke to us about yesterday. I lie down and within minutes I feel the back of my neck and feet being massaged. I quickly react and say I am not interested. It's dangerous even to ask, "how much?", as this indicates to the beach sellers that you are interested.

Cartagena Beach

I paddle a little way out into the water and take a shot of our hotel – the Hotel Dubai – with its extensive golden sails design, based on the famously iconic structure in Dubai. Reluctantly, we leave the water for terra firma and finalise our packing.

We have several hours before our flight to Bogotá takes off, and we hire a taxi driver to take us round Cartagena, taking in features of interest. Our taxi driver turns out to be a very knowledgeable guy with a pleasant manner, and he knows exactly where to take us.

Our first stop in the city is right outside the convention centre, which has a statue of two men posing in a water fountain. I have to confess that the point of the statue is unclear to me. But the stops become more meaningful to me at least. Shortly afterwards, we drive through a narrow arch into a cobbled area, bounded by battlements, on which are placed very rusty canon.

We climb up onto the battlements from where we overlook a harbour, with some very expensive floating real estate. A ship's horn sounds, emanating from a large container ship with the word HAMBURG written on its stern in huge capital letters. The ship slowly moves out towards the open sea. Maybe it brought some of the German sweets that Sylvia has been buying in the local shops to help her with her sore throat.

Cathedral, Cartagena Old City

Gabriel and Natalia in the Old City

Hotel Dubai, Cartagena

Our driver then takes us up a winding road to the crest of a hill – the Cerro Popal. Part of this hill was utilised by the Batteria San Juan, fortifications constructed to keep out the English who exhibited unkind intentions on the local population, probably during Tudor times. An information board refers to the batteria (gun battery) being constructed during the time of the Second English War, but I've no idea when that took place, what it was about, or even who won. I need to answer the call of nature, and the semi-hidden facility I am directed to is not much more than a hole in the ground. Mind you, I could have found it even if I had my eyes shut, as the smell is so pungent.

We are then driven to a market close to the main castle in the city – Castello San Felipe – apparently the first castle built by the Spanish in the New World. The market is full of hawkers; there's almost a continuous line of them, selling every wanted and unwanted item you can think of. And it's hot, at 33 degrees Celsius. The castle is massive, built in several layers of stone, and it looks impregnable; a huge bastion of strength when it was built in the sixteenth century.

Following in the footsteps of the conquistadores

Our next port of call is the Old City, in fact close to where we were last night. Our guide drives us past an impressive, colonial building with a long frontage where he tells us slaves were bought and sold. We also pass a former bullring which has been converted into a conference centre. I get the impression the Spanish love of bullfighting didn't really go down that well in the colonies, at least not here in Colombia. The Colombians took the enlightened view that bull fighting was unacceptable, and the 'sport' is now outlawed here.

Our evening flight to Bogotá is delayed by just over an hour and the activities and heat of the day are beginning to catch up with me. We touch down to a cold Bogotá and by the time we arrive at our hotel (the Wyndham again), I am struggling for breath like the last time I was here.

Gabriel and Natalia agree that we should rest in the morning and meet up again at 1pm. It sounds like a good plan to me.

Original Spanish Fort

Thursday 17 October
On the road to Melgar

Panoramic View of Cartagena

This morning, Sylvia, who has had a bad night, is not feeling well and she wonders whether she has shingles. After breakfast, she sleeps for a couple of hours. I ring Ed, our friend and next contact in Argentina, to confirm our visit to stay with him and his wife Marie. I realise we have problems with our flight from Salta to Buenos Aires at the end of our holiday, and this needs to be thought through.

We encounter another complication, this time over our hotel laundry service. By 11:00 hrs our laundry still hasn't arrived. When we ask about its delivery, we are informed that it will be with us tonight. But we are due to check out in a few hours' time and we remonstrate rather stridently over this. Eventually the laundry arrives in time, but it puts back our packing to make it a close-run thing to clear out of the room by the check-out time of 13:00.

At around twenty past one, Gabriel and Natalia collect us and we drive over to a huge shopping mall where we enjoy a late lunch. We are joined by Gabriel's sister, Ingrid, who has just finished work at her father's jeweller's shop for the day.

At around four in the afternoon, we leave Bogotá for Natalia's hometown of Melgar, which is a couple of hours away at a lower altitude where, we are forewarned, the temperature will be significantly hotter than here.

It's a tight squeeze in the car, with five people, our overnight bags plus our large suitcase, and not forgetting the wheelchair. Sylvia sits in the front, next to Gabriel who is the driver. Ingrid and Natalia have to slum it next to me in the back. Despite all the joking about Ingrid having a good appetite, she is slim enough for the three of us to fit comfortably in the back of what is an average-sized saloon car.

Pavement café, Cartagena Old City

We are travelling out of Bogotá on the principal highway to the south-west, and the rush-hour traffic conditions are challenging. It's two to three lanes of bumper to bumper, slow moving cars, buses, and heavy goods vehicles, whilst racing motorbikes create their own lanes, between the larger vehicles and on both sides of the highway; as many as five lines of bikes add to the chaos or excitement. The situation is complicated yet further by street hawkers, walking between the traffic, taking their life into their hands. One of these guys has a desperate look on his face; when we don't stop for him, he lashes out and hits the car with his red shirt. Gabriel says some of these guys try to cause an accident, so they can claim compensation. But I think the guy with the red shirt was deranged and near the end of his tether.

Gabriel points out a succession of shanty towns to our left, quite high up on the mountainside. He says they are the equivalent of the favelas of Brazil and are beyond the reach of normal services, such as proper sanitation and the rule of law.

The sun goes down to our right as we finally leave the huge city of Bogotá and drive through more rural, though not entirely depopulated areas. The highway is still quite busy and after reaching a summit maybe half an hour out of the city, it starts to make its way downwards continuously for the next hour or so, and it noticeably gets warmer. Even in the darkness, it is clear that the road is plunging through a rocky landscape.

Bogotá Traffic

At around the halfway point, we stop for a comfort break at a café called *The Laughing Cow* (*La Vaca que sourie*). But there is an acrid smell in this place, and we wonder whether the place should have been called *The Cow that Smells*.

The road towards Melgar continues to twist and turn through rocky terrain. Roadside signs warn of the danger of rock falls and the existence of geological fault lines. We pass close to very steep rock faces, and virtual overhangs are starkly visible in the car's headlights.

Later on, the two carriageways diverge, and our two lanes rapidly drop in altitude in a series of sharp curves. On one of these challenging bends, Gabriel is attempting to overtake a huge heavy goods vehicle, whilst at the same time keeping within the speed limit. Gabriel's manoeuvre is accompanied by the blaring of the horn of an impatient coach driver, who continues hooting until he finally overtakes both the lorry and us. Apparently, the opposite, Bogotá-based bound carriageway avoids many of these sharp bends as it progresses through a long tunnel.

We approach the town of Melgar past the main military base in Colombia, so Gabriel informs us. The base is segregated by a huge fenced-off area. Shortly after this, Gabriel turns off the main road and we enter the small settlement of Melgar, and within minutes we park outside the home where Natalia has lived for much of her life.

Looking down the road, we see an old lady sitting in a chair on the pavement by the entrance to the family home. No one needs to let us know that she is Natalia's grandmother, it is that obvious. Several more chairs spill out from the house onto the pavement. This is a street with a laid back, informal atmosphere, where neighbours walk in and out of each other's homes. Several mango trees have turned it into a leafy street; some of these trees are heavily laden with fruit.

The next hour is spent in convivial conversation with Natalia's parents, Raulfo and Liliena. As both of them are geography teachers, they invite me to ask them questions on the geography of Colombia. I start off by asking how easy it was for Colombia to stay together as a unit before and after its independence from Spain. They say the boundaries of Colombia were set by Spain as the colonial power and haven't changed since independence.

The part of Colombia which really wants to break away at the moment is Medellin, which considers it could be more prosperous on its own. I also ask about the transport systems in Bogotá and Medellin; they say Medellin has a much better transport system than Bogotá, with its metro and better airport links.

Raulfo and Liliena both retire in two years' time, and they tell me they want to visit all the countries in South America they have been teaching about. But Raulfo says he's not too keen to visit the USA, mainly for political reasons. They also want to visit Europe, including the UK. So, we give them a standing invitation to visit us when they make it to England, sometime in the next two plus years.

Later in the evening, we are taken to the pond at the nearest crossroads to Raulfo and Liliena's home. Here we can see several turtles, which come to life when bread is thrown into the water – and it gets even livelier when three ducks decide to swim over from the far side and take their pick.

At some time after nine o'clock, a collective decision is made to drive down into Melgar town centre and have a meal at a local pizzeria. It is still warm at this late hour, and the town centre is lively. The restaurant is a relaxing place and there is no shortage of conversation, and not just about Colombian geography. Virtually everyone opts for lasagne, which is excellent, but there is too much of it, and I am going to pay for this in the morning. Only after we return from eating out do we check in at the Melgar Resort Hotel, set in verdant surrounds, at around eleven at night. By now, Sylvia is exhausted, and we finally get to sleep around one in the morning.

Melgar street scene

Natalia's grandmother and family home, Melgar

Magdalena River

Our view from the penthouse suite, Cartagena

Friday 18 October
Colombia's Disappearing Railway Map And Other Matters

Locomotive 89 at Giradot

Unsurprisingly, we both oversleep, including right through my alarm. But yesterday was a full-on day. We just make it down to breakfast before it closes at ten o'clock. Gabriel and Natalia collect us around eleven and take us into the town centre, which comprises a few noisy and lively streets, arranged in blocks, with lots of small shops. Natalia finds a shop selling swimming costumes and before too long, Sylvia is kitted out for a date with a nearby water park.

Gabriel then drives us back to Natalia's parents' home, where lunch is laid on. I trot round the corner to take another look at the turtles, animals which I find fascinating. Several of them are resting on a muddy bank, just above the water's edge. I love watching these delightful creatures, and some of the bolder ones stare back at you, their facial features resembling that icon of the movies, ET. There are also several exquisitely coloured birds, something Colombia is really famous for.

Over lunch, we meet two friendly ladies from Upper New York State, from the town of Rochester, who are friends of Raulfo and Liliena. The younger one, who could be the daughter, called Elizabeth, works as an interpreter, which involves spending a lot of time in prisons and police stations; she says she loves the work, and that it's a job made in heaven for her.

View over the Sumepas River Valley

And then, as happened yesterday, a 'stranger' (to me at least), walks in off the street into the family home, and starts chatting to Natalia's grandmother. There is something magical and inclusive about this home and the relaxed movement of visitors.

In the afternoon, we drive to see Gabriel's brother, who is a pastor who lives close to the nearby town of Girardot, which seems to be the main economic centre of the local area. At one time, it was quite an important railway town, but more about that in a little while.

On the way, we call in at a drug store, where the pharmacist provides Sylvia with a mouth spray. She's in a lot of pain, and hopefully this new medication will get to the heart of the problem.

The main road to Girardot passes through an area of luxurious vegetation. We are in a broad valley, and some way to our left we can make out a high, rocky escarpment, which is a reminder that we are close to one of the mountain chains that forms part of the Andes range.

We pass a couple of high-rise holiday developments under construction alongside the main road. Gabriel says the area is popular with people living in Bogotá, wishing to live in more peaceful surrounds at the weekends. But the developments appear very urban to me and more of the same could compromise the very rural qualities that the city residents crave.

In the centre of Girardot stands a steam engine, locomotive number 89, of the Ferrocarriles Nacionais Giradotes. The name confirms the importance of Girardot on the historic railway map, when these impressive iron horses would haul express trains up and down Colombia. My recently purchased map of Colombia (dated 2018) shows the railway network as intact, although it does refer to landslides affecting a line over a hundred miles to the north-west. Despite the appearance of the railways on the map, it seems a sad fact that much of Colombia, in common with several other Latin American countries, no longer has a functional railway network, especially for long distance passenger trains.

Locomotive 89 is unlikely to ever move again, although it occupies pride of place, dominating the town centre. It is surrounded by a few railway tracks and what must be the remains of the town's railway station and possibly a freight yard. The hustle and bustle of the railway has been replaced by a level of tranquil dereliction, although several of the rail tracks are still in place and the demolishers haven't had it all their own way.

The disused tracks are still on the ground to the south, where the railway crosses the steep valley of the Magadalena River on its way to the Caribbean, several hundred miles further to the north. The railway crosses the river on a high steel bridge, and we are able to cross over on foot, walking on the tracks.

Looking down from the bridge there is a cluster of buildings in various stages of dereliction, some reduced to shells and many with smashed windows and no roofs. In some cases, the vegetation from the rain forest has broken through, with examples of trees growing up through the roofs of what were houses, sheds, and factories. It looks a strange environment. Gabriel says the ruins below are inhabited by people who are seen to be beyond the law, who prey on vulnerable people within the town. From what Gabriel says, I feel a measure of security from the fact that I am looking down on this 'bandit city' from a great height.

After walking through railway nostalgia, we visit Gabriel's brother, Miguel, who lives with his wife and two young daughters in the nearby town of El Espinal. Miguel gives us a warm welcome and invites us into his home. Miguel is a pastor in this town. Over our meal, he tells us that the surrounding area is relatively dangerous, with some families breaking up and in many cases, people are turning to a life of crime. He describes his ministry in this place as "difficult". He is a pastor under pressure.

We depart from Miguel and his little family as dusk falls. Gabriel makes good progress back to Melgar, passing - in many cases only gradually – lots of heavy goods vehicles. I get the impression that no one likes to be overtaken in Colombia! We arrive back in Melgar in the darkness. We take our evening meal in our hotel at around nine o'clock, and we are in bed by eleven; a relatively early night for us. There is loud thunder in the early hours, so we may be in for a wet Saturday.

Another view of the Sumepas Valley

Turtles at Melgar

Saturday 20 October
The Zoo and the Water Park

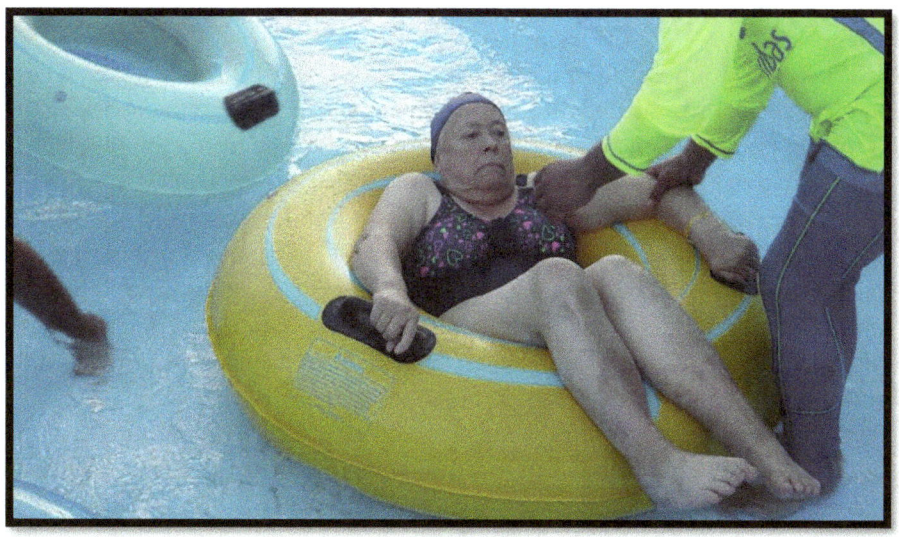

Sylvia about to get a wet launch – Melgar Water Park

Despite the thunder and rain, we sleep well and make it down to breakfast by 08:40. Over breakfast, we receive a 'What's App' message on my mobile phone from our son David, asking where a picture we sent him a short time ago, was taken.

"Bogotá" I say to him.

"Is that Colombia?"

"Yes"

"I've seen the place before – from a film on the drug lord, Pablo Escobar!"

'How to impress my kids without even trying', I smugly say to myself.

Our first expedition today is to a local zoo. This inspires Sylvia, for reasons best known to herself, to start singing the children's song: 'We're going to the zoo, zoo, zoo, how about you, you, you?' For some strange reason, this really appeals to Gabriel, who sings it, on and off, throughout the remainder of the morning. At this point, I am thinking that Sylvia has a lot to answer for.

The local zoo is well stocked, particularly with birds and small mammals, and not only with South American wildlife. It is verging on the impressive. The national bird of Colombia - the *Loros Colombianos* – is splendidly decked out in red, blue, and yellow, like the national flag, but it's clearly a bird with attitude and we witness a couple of stand-offs between these national birds.

We walk around a central lake, at one point passing a zip wire, where hapless guests are whizzed through the air above the lake and then back again. If it were possible, Sylvia would have loved to have attempted this, as she has no fear of these things. I am happy just watching.

After lunch and a short siesta, the plan for the afternoon is to visit a water park, where we have high hopes of getting Sylvia in the water. The staff at the park are very confident that they can transfer Sylvia from her wheelchair into a big rubber ring; this would mean that she could go for a water ride on the 'slow river'; this watery circuit flows at a fair pace, despite its name. The staff's confidence pays off, and before long, Sylvia appears in her swimming costume and sits in her rubber ring, with her legs dangling over the edge. She seems comfortable enough and clearly looking forward to the action.

Natalia and I clamber into our rubber rings, with the idea of keeping a close eye on Sylvia's progress through the waters. But my ring has a mind of its own, and I am quickly separated from the ladies. Before long, we sail (or float) into a tunnel where horrible things happen in the form of water cascading onto us from above. I do my best to slow down so Sylvia and Natalia can catch up with me, but to no avail.

At the end of the circuit, Sylvia decides it's so much fun that the three of us should go round the watery circuit together for a second time. This time I manage to get a grip on Sylvia's ring and the slow river circuit is completed in ship-shape fashion.

Then it's Gabriel and Ingrid's turn to navigate the slow river circuit and I decide to join them. Our passage degenerates into water fights and it's probably a good job that these rubber rings are unsinkable. As I try to extricate myself from my ring, I fall out completely in mercifully shallow water and Ingrid and Gabriel assist me to my feet. It's all good fun.

Natalia suggests we try the wave pool. We have to get a move on because there is only fifteen minutes to go before the sun sets completely. There's no time to admire the view if we are going to get kitted out in time. We are helped into our life jackets and we wade out into the pool towards the artificial waves.

Sylvia, sensibly in my opinion, sits this one out. Gabriel and I decide to go as far as the final wall, and at first all goes well. We make the wall successfully, our success being partly due to pushing others out of the way.

Then, as I turn to make it back to the shore, I become completely immersed by several high waves, and I take in quantities of water. I am now feeling less than comfortable. Gabriel spots my distress and shouts: "Mike, are you all right?" I reply: "No!" At this point a marshal appears out of nowhere, holding out a plastic bar for me to hold onto, and saying: "Tranquile!" ("be calm") and I am OK. Gabriel, who finds the whole incident hilarious, says he thought I was joking when I answered his question with a "No". It has certainly boosted my adrenaline level.

It is dark as we leave the pool area and head for the car. During the afternoon, a few people ask us where we are from and they all seem pleased when we say to them that we have Colombian friends. I guess we are too!

The plan is to travel back to Bogotá tomorrow, stopping over somewhere for lunch, with the possibility of seeing a tourist steam railway in the late afternoon. We spend the evening packing.

Interestingly, for once, it's the locals who have been attacked by mosquitoes-Natalia and Ingrid in particular have quite prominent bite marks on their legs and arms. Amazingly, Sylvia has got away with it Scot- free and I'm OK, so far as I know.

Melgar street scene

Sunday 21 October
The Best Laid Plans…

Gabriel and his brother Miguel – El Espinal

We have a sudden change of plan today. Gabriel's sister-in-law, Diana (Miguel's wife), has been taken ill, so the plan is now to go back to El Espinal to visit Diana's family, where we will drop off Ingrid to stay with them whilst Diana is in hospital. Ingrid is a trusted source of help and advice, and she will stay and assist here, and therefore will not return to work tomorrow.

After breakfast, there is time (just) to wheel Sylvia through part of the extensive landscaped grounds of this huge spa/hotel complex before being collected by Gabriel and Natalia. We check out and sign a card signifying we have no more to pay. It is essential that we keep this paper, we are told, as the security staff at the gate will ask for it. And they do.

On the way to El Espinal, Gabriel parks up by a roadside bar, to let Natalia, Ingrid and I walk back a short distance to a bridge over the Magdalena River, one of Colombia's main waterways. We look down on this river, flowing through a forested area. We can see a small vessel coming towards us on the river. This boat is known as a 'lancha', and it is a ferry, utilising this huge waterway. There are signs in the roadside bar advertising lancha trips from here to the nearest big town of Girardot.

We arrive in Gabriel's brother's town of El Espinal. We alight from the car and make our way to a nearby local food store, where we buy roast chicken, chips, and a couple of bottles of a local 'gassy' drink. The temperature has to be in the middle to upper thirties Celsius; sweat is pouring off me. We walk a couple of blocks to Miguel's home with our welcome food for everyone.

Even whilst we are relaxing at Miguel's home on a Sunday afternoon, there is a knock at the door, and it seems Miguel's pastoral duties are never finished. I notice an almost antique Singer sewing machine in the main room, an heirloom from the days when Britain was the workshop of the world.

Remains of Giradot Station

After we finish dinner, Sylvia is given another massage by Ingrid, which she really appreciates. I am given a hammock to rest in – this is a first for me – and my main problem now is trying to get out of it without crashing to the floor and killing myself.

The peace in the middle of the afternoon is shattered by loudspeakers blaring from slow moving vehicles, which are promoting different political parties and candidates for the post of regional mayor. We won't be seeing Ingrid again after we leave this peaceful home, as she is staying behind to look after Miguel's daughters whilst Diana is in hospital, undergoing treatment for peritonitis, so we say our goodbyes to her, and she gives us her e-mail address. It could be a good way of improving my Spanish, and we feel we have made a new friend.

Gabriel, Natalia, Sylvia, and I leave Miguel's home at around four in the afternoon. The main road back to Bogotá crosses the Magdalena River and passes through flattish countryside in the valley basin, much of it used for keeping cattle. Some of these animals have lumps on their backs like zebu cattle in Africa. Many of them are very thin, and some look emaciated. On both sides of the road, a few miles distant, there are continuous mountains with sharp peaks and steep sides. They form part of the Andean mountain chain which dissects Colombia from north to south. We can't see any snow on them, however.

We stop at a roadside store which is located next to a bridge over a small river, the Sumepas, which flows rapidly between large boulders. No doubt some of these rocks have been brought down from the mountains by the river in times of flood.

The Bogotá-bound carriageway of the main road passes through a large mountainous section via a tunnel. I'm not sure it was wise to point this out to Sylvia (who hates going through tunnels) earlier in the day, as she has been thinking about it ever since. The tunnel, however, is wide, well-lit and it is used only by north-bound traffic. It takes us only eight minutes to travel through it and Sylvia can enjoy the journey from hereon in.

Shortly after we emerge from the tunnel, with Sylvia still in one piece, we stop at a viewpoint which verges on the breath-taking. We take our drinks from a local café onto a viewing platform. From there, down in the middle distance, we can see the road we have just travelled on, emerging from the tunnel. Much further back, we can see the bridge over the River Sumepas, where we stopped some time ago. We have an extensive view of the river, flowing from left to right.

Above the Sumepas valley, there are magnificent rocky vistas to the left. This looks like wild territory, punctuated by several sheer rock faces. And there is no human habitation to be seen. Looking to the right, beyond the bridge, the valley leads to a distant landscape of buttes and mesas, reminding me of dramatic pictures I have seen of the rock formations in the Nevada desert. In the fading light, they look ethereal. I could stay at this amazing viewpoint for hours, taking in the outstanding beauty all around me and the majesty of this mountainous and remote terrain, but after half an hour or so, we set off on the road again.

Further on in the setting sun, we pass a string of settlements by the side of the highway, many of them linked to the tourist trade. Some basically advertise: "We have toilets" and nothing more. The ribbon development progressively intensifies as we approach the expansive greater Bogotá.

It is dark by the time we reach the edge of the city. A queue forms on the highway, and it takes us the best part of three hours to cross the city to Gabriel and Natalia's place. The highway conditions are chaotic. In addition to three lines of slow-moving cars, vans, buses and heavy goods vehicles, the gaps between the traffic lanes are filled by motorbikes. But the motorcyclists don't just stick to these gaps between the lines of vehicles; they often weave in and out of these lanes, presumably to gain ground on other vehicles. Then, to add to the chaos, there are lots of street sellers in the road. Some are of primary school age (if indeed they even go to school) and they walk between the slow-moving vehicles, holding out bottles of water and other drink and food items, and somehow avoiding being run over by the motor bikes.

Gabriel slows down and asks one of the street vendors a few questions, and he says he can tell by the vendor's accent that he is Venezuelan. Many Venezuelans perceive their country as a failed state and have voted with their feet to migrate to Colombia. Migration from Venezuela to Colombia is mostly illegal, and it is a big and growing problem for Colombia to handle, especially as it has a great amount of poverty-stricken inhabitants of its own. The atmospheric pollution on entering the vast urban area of Bogotá is visible and tangible.

At around nine in the evening, Gabriel decides to leave the congested highway and he drives through back streets to a part of the city called Galicia. We park opposite an illuminated five-a-side football ground, full of kids and adults playing, with lots of (relatively) joyful noise. There are a lot of people on the streets at this late hour (around ten o'clock).

"This is where we are living for the time being" Gabriel says. They are currently staying with Natalia's sister and her family until Gabriel and Natalia's home – apparently in the same neighbourhood - is ready for occupation. There is still some paperwork to do before they can move in. They invite us into their sister's house, and we enjoy cups of hot chocolate and something resembling a dessert version of Madeira cake, which tastes good.

We are back in our hotel by 11pm and our next task is to recover the laundry order we made a few days ago when we were last staying here. There is quite a lot of rearranging to do after a reminder or two, and the laundry is eventually delivered to our door. We finally get to bed with two nearly packed suitcases lying on the floor.

Natalia, Gabriel, Mike and Sylvia at Sumepas viewpoint

Monday 22 October
Flying over the Amazon Rainforest

Flying over Amazonas

Neither of us is feeling particularly good this morning and getting out of bed is a major challenge for both of us. The plan is to make our separate way to the airport and meet Gabriel and Natalia there, where we will say a final goodbye to them. They send messages to our mobiles saying they are stuck in "many traffic".

We take the hotel bus and eventually meet up with Gabriel and Natalia at the airport in the departure lounge. We spend a few final moments sharing together, and thanking them for their constant companionship over these last ten days, for showing us so much of their beautiful country and letting us have the privilege of meeting their parents, relatives and other wonderful Colombian people. And for just being our friends.

Eventually, we have to drag ourselves away from Gabriel and Natalia and meet up with our wheelchair pushing staff at 12:00 noon on the dot, or "en punto" as they say in these parts. Once on our Airbus 320, bound for Buenos Aires, we have a wait of 40 minutes before taking off into a wet and cloudy Bogotá sky. But as soon as we fly above the clouds, we experience bright sunshine and our world changes dramatically.

It's not long before the clouds have disappeared and we can see clearly that we are flying over an extensive rain forest, stretching as far as the eye can see. The eastern part of Colombia makes up the westernmost part of the Amazon Rain Forest – known in Colombia as 'Amazonas'. It's a big part of Colombia. And we are flying over it. Several rivers reflect the sunlight as they weave their incredible meandering patterns across the green velvet below.

Then we fly over a river that is much bigger than all the others, with islands and sandbanks, even beaches. Could this be the Amazon? I ask myself. This part of the rainforest that we are overflying appears to be largely intact and magnificent.

Another river has meandered so much that it has left behind at least six oxbow lakes that I can see. I confess that, although learning about oxbow lakes all those decades ago in school geography lessons, I have never actually seen one before. It's like buses – I never see one and then six come along in a row! I just can't take my eyes off the magnificent beauty set out below me.

Sylvia is glued to an Andre Rieu CD via her headphones. The songs on the CD include *Don't cry for me, Argentina...* Is someone trying to tell us something?

Over a period of around two hours, we fly over dozens of water courses. Most of them (except perhaps the largest) display the most elaborate meanders and flow patterns. It is a privilege to look down on such a relatively undisturbed and beautiful area. My only problem is that the light refraction on the glass of the plane window is probably going to play havoc with the quality of my photographs.

And then I spot it – a fire. And then another fire, spewing billows of smoke over a wide area. Paradise lost. Now we are flying over an area with decidedly less forest cover. I feel depressed at the wanton destruction of the rain forest below me. We fly over square shaped, artificial looking bodies of water, presumably linked to agriculture. This looks like ranching country, driven by the ever-increasing global demand for beef burgers, primarily from the West. Then more fires. I'm getting really depressed now.

We fly into a magnificent sunset before it is subsumed into pink 'cotton wool' as the clouds envelop us. After breaking free above the clouds, we can see a striking red glow on the horizon with the most amazing cloud shapes making improbable forms before the whole scene is overtaken by darkness. I put my camera away and stick my head into Sebastian Faulks' *'Paris Echo'* for the rest of the flight.

Nearing the end of the flight, I look down onto a huge oil field in the sea, with interconnected platforms, illuminating the night. These artificial structures seem to extend for miles. Shortly afterwards, we drop down and land at Buenos Aires International Airport.

We encounter a pleasant experience in the arrivals hall at the airport – we see a lady holding up a card saying 'Mr and Mrs Fox' – and it is for us! The lady's name is Mariana. She greets us and takes us to her car, where we meet Christian, the driver.

On the main road into the city centre, we agree to go on a tour of Buenos Aires tomorrow. Even at eleven at night, we experience traffic congestion once we come off the airport highway and drive into the city centre.

Our hotel, the Pulitzer, is a welcoming place, located in a narrow street (Calle Maipu) just off the dominant Avenida 9 de Julio in the city centre.

After we are settled in our room, I venture across the street to a restaurant and order sandwiches, a mug of hot chocolate and a bottle of coke, and take it back to share with Sylvia.

We finally unpack a little and we are in bed around 02:00 hrs. It's been a long day.

Tuesday 23 October
Exploring Buenos Aires

Mausoleum of Jose de San Martin

Just before eight in the morning, my mobile phone rings. It's my boss, Simon on the other end of the line. "Are you OK?" he asks. I am trying to work out why I am receiving a work call at this early hour when I am on holiday. Is this the prelude to a disciplinary action? What on earth have I done? He then says: "I am ringing you to congratulate you; you have been promoted!" I remember the interview I attended several months ago, where I thought I had messed up big time. I clearly didn't mess up to the extent I thought I had! I thank Simon and chew over the implications. For one thing, it would be a tad churlish if I were to announce that I aim to retire in a couple of months' time, as I was thinking of doing. Anyway, it's something to think about over the last few days of our holiday.

Our guide, Mariana, collects us from our hotel at 11 o'clock, and we just about make it on time. Our first place to visit is the impressive square in the city centre – the Plaza de Mayo – where the Argentinian rebellion against Spain, the colonial power at that time, really kicked off, with the first rebellion in 1810, and as the square declares, in May of that year. Independence, however, had to wait for another six years and only came about through a lot more fighting. The square is impressive, not because of its size, although it is by no means small, but because it has a great atmosphere.

The square is fronted by beautiful, traditional buildings, including the classically colonnaded Metropolitan Cathedral (also known as the Iglesia de Santisima Trinidad – Church of the Holy Trinity - which somehow sounds more impressive in Spanish). The current Pope Francis, who comes from Argentina, presided in this cathedral before going on to higher things.

The Plaza de Mayo is the official centre of this city of nearly three million inhabitants (not forgetting several times that number in the adjoining areas, making this one of the largest conurbations in the Americas). And the square has a city centre feel to it.

Plaza de Mayo, Buenos Aires

Magdalena River from former railway bridge, Giradot

Open air tango, La Boca

Looking to the left from the cathedral entrance, the Casa Rosada occupies the eastern end of the square. This lovely, iconic, pink building is a Government palace. This is where Eva Peron addressed the crowds in the tumultuous times of the nineteen forties and fifties. The palace is now gated off, with the aim of preventing modern day demonstrations. And this is a sensitive period, with a general election in a few days' time, and maybe another 'peronista' will gain office again.

There are also bandanas set out on the floor of the square, in memory of the 'Disappeared' – all the people who protested against a former regime and who haven't been seen again. The background and perhaps key issue to the general election is inflation running at 50% per annum, whilst last month's rate (September) spiked at 6%. These are worrying times for Argentina. Although the city centre still retains an affluent, sophisticated feel to it, there are disconcerting signs that all is not well, such as empty shops and homeless people on the streets. Even the most foreign of visitors to the city cannot fail to notice all the election posters; they are literally everywhere.

The other really eye-catching structure in this amazingly impressive square is the white marble obelisk or pyramid, sitting in the middle of the plaza, built to celebrate the freedom that Argentina won after casting off Spanish colonial rule. It has a slender elegance, and to my mind it fits in with the rest of the square – it almost pulls the rest of the square in towards it – without overpowering its setting. Quite a fine balance, which I think they have got right. Not surprisingly, it is known as the 25th of May Pyramid.

La Boca, Buenos Aires

Mariana takes us inside the vast cathedral, and we enter in the middle of a mass being celebrated in honour of the Buenos Aires federal police force. It looks like every seat is taken, and there are rows of police officers standing everywhere you look. This is maybe not the best moment to try and manoeuvre with a wheelchair!

We slowly push our way towards the huge mausoleum in one wing of the cathedral, which houses the tomb of General José de San Martin, the liberator of Argentina from Spanish rule, and the man whose statue we will encounter in almost every town in which we travel in this country. He seems to have assumed a god-like status in this nation, at least on a level with Simon Bolivar in Colombia.

Buenos Aires is known as the Paris of South America and it's not difficult to see why. There are some wide boulevard type thoroughfares and many of the elegant nineteenth century buildings would not look out of place in Paris. This really is a beautiful city, at least in the centre of the metropolis.

Casa Rosada, Buenos Aires

Christian drives us to a fascinating area of the city, which is a cross between London's Dockland and Covent Garden. This is La Boca. It is a crowded meeting place of the rich and poor, and nowadays it is a tourist trap. There are brightly coloured tenement buildings, including painted brick and metal, producing an almost kaleidoscopic effect. We walk/push past a couple of tango demonstrations on the street, where the dancers pose for photographs, in between the 'action'. We wander through a street market, and I buy a painting from a local artist, depicting two boats with stylish narrow funnels in the harbour, for 15 US dollars.

The Boca football stadium comes into view, and on the opposite side of the road there is a huge mural depicting a footballer by the name of Carlos Tevez, who now plays for Boca. In a former life, he played for both the Manchester clubs (first United and then City), and I am looking forward to seeing him playing when I view a big screen in a restaurant on the next match night. In fact, I find out that the next match night is this evening, when Boca will be at home to River Plate, their local rivals, for the semi-final, second leg of the South America cup.

Children in La Boca

Mariana tells us that last year, the local rivalry between these two clubs spilt over into violence and mayhem on the pitch. This resulted in another failed attempt to organise a peaceable match, after which the game was held in Madrid!! I have never heard anything like it. I notice the barricades around the roads leading to the stadium, which have been erected by the police to separate the rival fans.

Christian pulls up at a nearby street café, situated next to a freight railway; there's some doubt as to whether the line is still in use, although Christian thinks he saw a locomotive on the track a few weeks ago. More Boca fans, waving their blue and yellow scarves, walk past us as we drink our cokes at an 'outside' table in the street.

Christian then collects us in his people carrier and we drive off. After about five minutes, I ask him if Mariana is coming with us. He exclaims something that I can't understand, laughs, trying not to sound nervous, and then races back to the café to collect her. Mariana, whom we collect from the café we were in, is not a 'happy bunny' right now, as we would say in the UK.

Sylvia, our guide Mariana and our driver Christian, at a café in La Boca

Café/Studio in La Boca

Our next port of call is a dockside regeneration scheme, which goes by the name of Puerto Maduro. It looks something like the Salford Quays regeneration scheme in Greater Manchester. Apparently, these docks eventually could not handle the really big container ships, which have now been relocated to new, purpose-built docks constructed on the edge of the

River Plate, a short way to the south. The warehouses lining the quaysides were trading in wheat, corn and timber which were delivered from the exporter countries of the world.

The business district in this area changed 30 years ago into a new upmarket residential neighbourhood, whilst the channels from here to the sea became too small for modern shipping. Even the abandoned grain silos are making way for, or being converted into, expensive condos in this new desirable residential area.

The water is now home to yachting and rowing activity, so the docks are busy again but with pleasure as the main theme. One of the waterways is graced by an elegant Calatrava pedestrian bridge, giving the neighbourhood a real touch of class. There's even a floating casino, which is maybe not the ideal location in which to be if you have just lost a fortune on the gambling tables.

Mariana agrees to take us to the Estacion Retiro, Buenos Aires' huge central railway terminus built partly by a British architect, Richard Prentice in 1903. Its façade is imposing, again with a Parisian feel to it (as with so much in this city), and the high and expansive train shed over the platforms and tracks is atmospheric. You can almost feel the smoke and noise of the early steam locomotives as they would have puffed and clanked into this station, which still exudes real charm. The present-day trains, blue diesel multiple units, mostly only a few carriages long, seem out of scale in this cathedral of celebration to rail travel.

Maybe coming here in the middle of the day, away from the rush hour is the explanation for a sense of anti-climax from the heady, pre-war days, but there are few trains at this hour, and they almost look lost in this enormous superstructure. I count only eight, amply well spaced-out platforms, although I gather there are in fact three stations sitting next to each other, each with their separate layout of tracks fanning out in different directions. But this one – the Retiro - is the symbol of the great optimism that the country expressed in its railways in a bygone era, which appears to have ended or at least declined with the post-war economic turbulence and the Peronista era.

Situated in a park, facing the station, stands a clock tower, which until the Falkands War was known as the English Tower, as it was a gift to Argentina from Great Britain in 1910. There is also a stainless-steel sculpture of a flower – the 'flora generica', named to represent all flowers. When the machinery is working, the flower opens and closes impressively, so I'm told.

Dockland Regeneration, Puerto Madero, Buenos Aires

We make our way through central Buenos Aires, a city resplendent with statues, one of which stands in honour of the city's most famous daughter, Eva Peron. We are in the verdant and expensive looking neighbourhood of Recoleta, where the buildings, several of them embassies, again have a strong French influence, a recurring theme in Buenos Aires. There are many restaurants and what I would term up-market nightclubs.

Puerto Madero

Also, in this neighbourhood we come across a huge cemetery, replete with buildings, some as high as houses, giving it the aura of the city of the dead. But it's a must-see area for many tourists. This necropolis contains several streets, extending over an area of six hectares (about 15 acres), with some graves and funereal buildings dating back to 1822.

Mariana informs us that there are many family graves, with around 4,800 tombs, plus underground galleries, some of which go down for two levels. The most famous occupant in this cemetery must be Eva Peron, but many dignitaries have come here for their final resting place, including several ministers of war. There is also a grave commemorating an interesting Irishman, William Brown, credited with the founding of the Argentine navy.

The ladies finally succeed in dragging me away from this interesting cemetery and back to the reality of the land of the living, and Mariana says she knows a perfect restaurant for us, just round the corner. It's called the 'Las Nazarinas' restaurant, where Mariana leaves us for the day. Like many eating places in Argentina, it serves excellent steak at amazingly reasonable prices. I opt for tender loin (lomo) and really enjoy it. Sylvia, however, finds that the quantity of meat on her plate exceeds her capacity to consume and she feels guilty leaving so much uneaten on her plate. I have no such problems in this department.

Sylvia and I make our way back to our hotel at around four in the afternoon. The hotel is about four blocks away from the restaurant, so we don't need a taxi. It has been hot all day, and it's just starting to cool down slightly, pleasant weather for walking.

Entrance to Buenos Aires Cemetery

But the day is far from over for us. At half past six, we are collected by coach from our hotel to go out for a dinner and tango evening, something I signed up to rather half-heartedly. We leave the coach and enter the venue via a dark entrance, illuminated by a number of photographs featuring tango dancing scenes. These pictures make quite an impact, giving out a promise of something exotic to follow. Will this put me off my dinner? Probably not.

In the dining area, which is also low-lit, there is a raised stage to our left. On this platform are placed a lone guitar and a gramophone, á la *His Master's Voice*, possibly dating from the pre-war era.

Inside the City of the Dead

25th of May Pyramid, Plaza de Mayo, Buenos Aires

Then the show begins. There is a band, comprising piano, double bass, concertina, and guitar – and of course lots of dancers. The tango, as everyone knows, is the national dance of Argentina. I am free to photograph lots of long legs (belonging to mostly beautiful and universally quite tall female dancers), and some atmospheric and beautiful dancing. There is one particularly lively act, involving tap dancing with skipping over ropes, and another scene set around traditional gas streetlamps. Considering most acts don't have drums, the dancing is very rhythmic and pulsating. Even the occasional acts which feature just the musicians are captivating. I have to admit that I am enjoying this more than I had expected.

As we depart from the venue back to the waiting coach, a black guy helps Sylvia step up, out of her wheelchair and into our vehicle. He tells me he's from French Guiana (Cayenne), and informs me that there aren't many blacks in Buenos Aires. I ask him how comfortable he feels out here. "Not too good", he says, "I aim to return to Cayenne soon".

Our coach driver taking us back to our hotel has the Boca-River 'derby' football game on his radio. Even the commentators don't appear to be agreeing with each other. We observe that there are a lot of police about on the city's streets; tension and excitement are in the air.

Once in the hotel, I switch on the television and catch the last 25 minutes of the Buenos Aires football derby game. Boca have to score two goals to level the match and wipe out the lead that River have from the first leg. They manage to score one from a powerful header, connecting from a free kick to halve the deficit. But press as they do, Boca fail to score the all-important second goal and River survive to go through to the next round of the South America Cup. In the process, the referee lets a lot of Boca fouls go unpunished, and he seems to have forgotten where he has put his cards.

We finish our re-packing and are in bed by one in the morning. It's been a long day, but a full and interesting one

Tango evening

Street art, La Boca

Wednesday 23 October
Travelling to Northern Argentina

Station Face, Estacion Retiro, Buenos Aires

Sylvia is awake at three in the morning with a mouth ulcer which is hurting. She says she needs hot water, so I trot down to the guy on reception, who seems glad of the company in the small hours. He walks into the hotel kitchen and pours hot water into a Styrofoam. Sylvia rallies after this, but we both lose a lot of sleep.

We are down to breakfast by nine, a bit later than we had planned. Then we try to send money to Gabriel and Natalia in Colombia, in lieu of hotel and airline payments. But one company, after promising us an instant money transfer, says it is experiencing technical issues and pulls out. Another company isn't answering the phone number I have been given. As a result, we run out of time to walk round the block, and we have to hurry back to our hotel.

At twelve noon, our guide Mariana collects us from the hotel, and Christian is our driver again; our team is reunited. Christian seems pleased to see us again. Mariana says she is confident that we can take a boat trip on 29 October when we return to Buenos Aires after spending a few days with friends in the far north of Argentina.

Mariana drops us off at the regional airport, where we are booked onto an internal flight to Salta. There we will spend two nights before making the six-hour road trip up to the small (verging on tiny) town of Tartagal, which is a further hour's drive to the Bolivian border. We have to pay extra for our heavy baggage, even though we are only taking one case between us (having left the other one temporarily at our hotel in Buenos Aires). But the airport officials are a cheery bunch. At security, one of them says I can't take my nougat bar with me, and then laughs. What a tease! It is clear, however, that some officials are happier than others, mainly depending on whether their side won or lost in last night's football match. In footballing terms, this is a divided city.

Station ceiling

Inside the station

Shortly after our plane takes off, we catch a great view of the area known as the Delta, where several waterways, including the Parana River, join to form a water lattice, before flowing into and becoming the mighty Rio de la Plata (River Plate) a few miles downstream. It's a green landscape down there and, unsurprisingly, quite flat. Further on, I spot one ocean going ship on an inland waterway, and some of the towns along its route have docks and commercial areas, showing how important the seaway is to the local economy.

Around two hours later, the plane almost glides over a wide, flat valley, defined by Andean cordilleras. The contrast between the flatness of the valley floor and the high, craggy mountains is stark but the valley looks enchanting. A few farmsteads can be spotted in the valley. The city of Salta (with half a million inhabitants) is still somewhat distant, and the airport itself has the feel of a large farmstead set in rural surrounds.

We experience a minor incident at the airport. Sylvia is wheeled down but not on her own personal wheelchair. But her wheelchair doesn't arrive on the baggage reclaim. Eventually, we are sitting in a steadily emptying room, with nothing left on the carousel, which then shuts down. There is no-one around. There are no more planes taking off or landing. After half an hour, I look outside the main entrance, and there, sitting next to the taxi rank, is the recalcitrant wheelchair. I can almost sense it saying to me: "What took you so long?"

Our taxi driver takes us along quiet, rural roads for about 30 minutes. It is a pleasant, sunny day, and we have clear views of the mountains on both sides of the valley. The driver says that out here, life is more tranquil than in Buenos Aires, and it's clear which place he prefers. It is no exaggeration to say that there is almost no traffic on these roads – at least not until we enter the city of Salta, where it is a tad congested in places.

Salta's historic city centre has some attractive and interesting architecture, and the driver stops briefly in the main square (plaza principal), which looks like something out of eighteenth-century Spain.

Our hotel, the Sheraton Salta Hotel, is situated about halfway up a hillside. Our fourth-floor room has a panoramic view of the city, with its mountainous backdrop.

We haven't been in the hotel long before Sylvia is feeling unwell again. She is finding eating quite painful, and it appears to be the same situation as she experienced in Cartagena, where the doctors only prescribed a three-day course of antibiotics. We talk to the people on reception, and they confirm that they have a specialist medical emergency team. Just after finishing our evening meal, we are visited in our hotel room by a doctor and his assistant, who has a squeaky high voice. Then one of the receptionists, who can speak acceptable English, joins us. But the doctor speaks at such a fast pace that he leaves the receptionist floundering in her attempts to interpret. The whole scene is quite amusing, and at one point, the doctor asks me if I can understand him without the need to go via the receptionist, but I can't cope with his rapid Spanish either!

Eventually, the doctor manages to tell Sylvia that she should take medication for pneumonia because he is hearing strange sounds through his stethoscope. But Sylvia refuses, because this clashes with advice she has received in a recent consultation back in the UK. This leads to the inevitable form filling; Sylvia has to sign so as to indicate that if she succumbs to pneumonia, it is entirely her responsibility.

I get chatting to one of the receptionists, a young lady by the name of Sol several times this afternoon and evening. She tells me that she is sitting environmental law exams next week and has set her sights on becoming a lawyer. "We kind of base our law on your Magna Carta", she says. I guess that is so.

We enjoy a beautiful sunset over the city from our bedroom window, and we are asleep before midnight.

View of Salta from Sheraton Salta Hotel

View of Salta from the summit

View of Salta from cable car

Park in Salta

Thursday 24 October
Exploring Salta

Our friends Ed and Marie Brice, whom we will be visiting in the far north of Argentina tomorrow, have advised us to take a day looking around the colonial city of Salta and its beautiful architecture. We have adopted this advice and today is the day to explore this city.

However, our day starts with communication difficulties. Firstly, I can't get through to my friend Ed in Tartagal using my mobile phone. I ask a friendly hotel receptionist if he could try and make contact with Ed on the hotel phone, but he can't get through to him either. Then I have an unimpressive, uninspirational thought. Why not use his landline? And I get through to him immediately! We agree that I should hire a taxi tomorrow, leaving our hotel in Salta at 2pm and then book to stay in the same hotel when we return to Salta on the night of the 28th, so it will be a straightforward task to book a taxi from the hotel to Salta airport on 29 October (and then on to Buenos Aires). Ed also kindly agrees to drive us back from Tartagal to Salta on 28 October. So, things are sorted for our remaining time in northern Argentina.

Sylvia and I venture out of our hotel mid-morning, with me pushing the wheelchair. It looks like it's downhill all the way to the city centre and our plan is to book a taxi back to the hotel when we feel we have had enough walking/pushing/being pushed. We also aim to go for a trip on the cable car which we gather takes people to the top of one of the mountainous sides of the valley, overlooking the city. But our initial journey, pushing the wheelchair, involves a string of hazards, especially for Sylvia in the wheelchair. There are virtually no dropped kerbs, with significant drops down from the pavement to the carriageway of the road. Many of the pavements are pockmarked with potholes, and the slopes are often steep. This really is a minefield for disabled travel.

At one intersection, the angles and slope catch us out, and in trying to rectify a hazardous situation, Sylvia ends up out of the wheelchair and on the road. Fortunately, she is OK, and as I try and get her back into the wheelchair, immediately three men appear, seemingly out of nowhere. Between us, we set Sylvia back into her wheelchair. One of the men asks where we are going and I say the pharmacist which has been recommended by the hotel. "Get in the car!" he says, and he drives us there, right to the doorstep. Again, we experience an act of kindness when we least expect it.

Once inside the pharmacy, I give the pharmacist the prescription that the doctor gave us in our hotel the night before. He looks at the sheet of paper, and then he says firmly, "No!" I am non-plussed and clearly appear to him to be confused at what he is telling me. Eventually, I get from him that he does not have any of the medication we need in stock and then we both see the funny side of my misunderstanding. He tells me that there is another pharmacist, called La Vallee, just two blocks away, and advises us to make our way there, which we do.

We find the La Vallee pharmacy as directed. The woman serving us asks where we are from, and then says she is keen to practise her English. She says: "I teach you Spanish and you teach me English!" It sounds like a good deal to me. And, perhaps even of greater importance, she has the medication that Sylvia needs.

We walk a short distance in the ever increasing heat, along a road with a name which celebrates the bi-centenary of the Battle of Salta, which was one of the main battles in the war of liberation, won by Argentina's hero, General José de San Martin.

We find a street café, which looks friendly and relaxed and it turns out to be so. Sylvia orders a tostada, which is OK but, as she says, it is very salty – but I inform her that we are eating in the city which has the Spanish name for salt, so is it any surprise! When I pay the bill, they ask me to write down my passport number on the invoice. When I say I haven't got my passport with me, the waitress says that it's quite OK – just write down your phone number! I love the people's laid-back attitude out here towards bureaucracy!

From the café, we catch a taxi to the central park – the Parque de San Martin (who else?). This is where the cable car starts from. Our driver asks where we are from, and when we tell him, he says he loves English music, and to prove his point, so he says, he proceeds to insert a CD of Diana Ross, who of course is an American singer! But I guess she is singing in English. In our experience, he's not the first person out here in Argentina to spontaneously say something favourable about Britain, which is an unexpected surprise on our travels.

The taxi drops us off at the entrance to the cable car ticket office. A very friendly guy there asks us if we speak English, and then advises that right now, there is an event taking place at the cable car destination, which will restrict our viewing opportunities. He says it would be much better if we returned to the booking office later in the afternoon, say at four o'clock.

We heed his good advice and look around the Parque de San Martin, which surrounds the cable car base. The park has few flower beds or pleasant grassy areas; in fact, it has nothing much to write home about – except for a large statue of General José de San Martin, astride a horse in rampant position on its hind legs, with a plaque saying that the statue was financed by the people of La Paz (presumably in Bolivia).

Summit Café, Salta

The park accommodates several semi-concealed or at least low-profile areas, which are occupied by young couples, still in their school uniforms, presumably practising their English irregular verbs......

Sylvia fancies buying a hat from the local market, but we need to access some more pesos from a local cash point before the hat, one which she has already spotted and earmarked for herself, becomes hers. But it's clear that she has already made her mind up, and I need to find the money.

After strolling/pushing for a while, we catch a taxi back towards the cable car station. Our driver asks where we are from, and when we state the UK, he starts talking about the Malvinas! (He is the first person on our travels in Argentina to do so.) He's quite friendly, and I think he just wants a discussion, but I am careful not to get too involved. As he stops to let us out, he shows me a 50 peso (I think) note, which is covered by a map of the islands that make up the Malvinas! (Or the Falkland Islands if you take the British position on their sovereignty, but clearly, writing a travel diary in Argentina, this is something I couldn't possibly comment on.)

Another view of Salta from cable car

Just after 4pm, we return to the cable car station. The ramps to and from the gondolas are really steep, and in both directions, young men come up to us and ask if they can help push the wheelchair.

We are installed in our own gondola, complete with Sylvia's collapsed wheelchair. It takes about ten minutes to be transported through the air to the side of a mountain overlooking the city of Salta. The built-up area of the city occupies virtually the whole of a relatively flat valley floor with a huge range of mountains on the opposite side.

The area at the top of the cable car ride has some steep inclines, but it's just about manageable for pushing Sylvia in the wheelchair. We find a well patronised café which commands a great view over the city and enjoy a coffee. Next to the cable car summit, there are two imposing religious statues standing guard and overlooking Salta. One of them sports a halo, but its aura is somewhat tarnished by rust and is generally covered by irreligious deposits from passing birds.

Salta is looking resplendent in the early evening sunshine. Its grid iron street pattern comes across clearly, and it has almost no really high tower blocks. It looks settled and peaceful from up here on the edge of a mountain. Some of the 'avenidas' really are avenues, as they are lined with many mature trees, which add to the city's verdant ambience. Its mountainous backdrop gives the city an extra dimension, and many of its colonial buildings are still standing. Later in the year the mountains will be snow covered.

As we leave the cable car, which is known as the Teleférico San Bernardo, we head for the market. Once there, Sylvia, unsurprisingly decides to buy a hat, or sombrero as the market seller calls it, although it's not the one she originally spotted. Sylvia plays a hard bargain, refusing two offers of 250 pesos before agreeing to a purchase of 200 pesos. This girl will go far.

Delta Scene

Another scene from the Delta

Friday 25 October
The Trek to Tartagal

Much of the morning is spent trying to overcome a technical problem with transferring money, which is only partly solved. I also write a few post cards, which is quite late in the day, really. We are highly likely to arrive home first.

We book a taxi driver to take us up to visit our friends Ed and Marie, who live in the remote town of Tartagal, situated in the northernmost part of Argentina, next to the Bolivian border. It's around 220 miles to the north of Salta, and our taxi ride is going to take us around six hours. Everyone at the hotel here in Salta tells us that up in Tartagal, it is really hot. And we are thinking that it's pretty hot here in Salta!

Sometime around two in the afternoon, our taxi arrives at the hotel. The driver is friendly, which bodes well for quite a long journey at close quarters. He says he doesn't know exactly where our friends live in Tartagal, but we have their address, and he seems pretty confident that it will work out OK. It is about 30 degrees Celsius as we drive away from the hotel and on to the main road network.

Crossing a river en route to Tartagal

The dual carriageway out of Salta quickly reduces to a single lane in each direction, although the road surface is generally adequate. Traffic levels are moderate, and we don't get caught up in any congestion. Much of our journey passes between fields of sugar cane; some of it is burning, with billows of thick smoke rising into the hazy sky. The remains of a railway, running parallel to the highway, are clearly visible to our right, which is a sad sight for a railway nerd like me. We are informed that much of the railway track was swept away in recent floods, and it seems that there hasn't been the political or economic will to reconstruct the line. Whether this railway will ever be resurrected into a working line again is anybody's guess, but it's probably unlikely.

We cross several dry and almost dry rivers, and our driver informs us that the British-built railway bridges survived the recent floods intact, whereas the corresponding road bridges were largely swept away. The railway bridges, still standing with hardly a blemish, strike me as impressive steel structures. It's a shame the rest of the railway wasn't built to the same high standard.

On our left we can see the Andean chain of mountains, rising up steeply from the plain, maybe about 20 miles distant. Our driver, Anibal, is quite communicative, and we teach each other Spanish and English words and generally get along fine.

We pull in off the main road and stop at a roadside café for refreshment and a comfort break. We also appreciate the welcome cool temperature from the café's air conditioning system. Sylvia, true to form, makes friends with a stray dog. Outside the café, the quite pungent smell pervading the place is coming from a nearby molasses factory. Ignoring the terrible aroma, there are great views across the sugar cane fields on the opposite side of the main road to the foothills of the Andes; the landscape seems to change from flat to mountainous in an instant, although distance plays tricks on the eyes. The smell, however, is quite overwhelming and I am glad when we resume our journey. The increase in the temperature after Salta is also noticeable, and we are only halfway to Tartagal.

Further to the north, the landscape becomes greener. There are banana trees, orange groves, and apple and mango trees, to name a few features in the landscape. The rivers we cross have water flowing in them, in some cases more convincingly than in others – until, interestingly, we cross the Rio Seco, which as its name in Spanish suggests, is completely dry.

Anibal is good company as we continue to teach each other words from our mother tongues. This state of affairs lasts until we pull into a service station for fuel, and he says something to me in Spanish like "subir del carro". I am a little tired by this time, several hours into the journey, and after he repeats his instruction to me a couple of times and gets no response, he shouts at me in English "Get out of the car!" This rouses me out of my semi-comatose state and amuses him greatly, and the reason, apparently, is because his car is fuelled on natural gas, and it is therefore necessary for everyone to get out.

Statue of Jose de San Martin in Plaza San Martin, Tartagal

We need to stop again at another filling station, and Anibal hugely enjoys shouting at me again: "Get out of the car!" before chuckling. The car needs to refuel three times on our journey, such is the requirement for natural gas users. But we are in a region which apparently has huge reserves of the stuff, so I guess there's no danger of the service stations around here running out of the commodity any time soon.

Roadside signs warn that in heavy rain, the road will be flooded. Apparently, one of the biggest 'offenders' is the River Pilcomayo, which floods most years, as it sheds water gathered in the Bolivian uplands. We also pass through a couple of police roadblocks, which are set up, so we are informed, to attempt to intercept the flow of drug traffic from Bolivia.

We also negotiate a number of hazards in the road. On one occasion, a fox shoots across the road just in front of us. The next problem is several cows in the highway, but Anibal is able to skilfully weave a safe passage through the herd.

Our taxi reaches the edge of Tartagal at the close of the day and it starts to turn dark. Anibal's GPS guides us to our friends' address without too much difficulty. Our friends Ed and Marie are sitting outside the main entrance to a missionary compound, surrounded by high walls, which is their home. As Anibal drives away, he winds down his window and shouts: "Get out of the car!" We need to explain the reason for this strange remark to Ed and Marie.

It's good, at the end of a long journey, to unwind over a meal with our good friends. Ed, who is English, is the pastor of the local Anglican church in Tartagal, and he is also involved with befriending local Indian communities (they don't seem to be referred to as 'first nations' here), including helping them with trading ventures, land rights and advice over development and flooding issues. His wife Marie is from Argentina, but until fairly recently, they were both working among Indian communities in Paraguay.

Landscape on the outskirts of Tartagal

During our meal, Ed drops a bombshell by asking me if I would preach at his church on Sunday! (i.e., in less than two days' time.) He says that he expects that I have brought plenty of material with me for preaching purposes (no, not true), but I agree to do it, and Ed says he will interpret for me. It's good to eat and chat about all manner of things, and there is no shortage of conversation, but I will have to think hard about a message and write it all down tomorrow!

We are asleep shortly after midnight.

Ed and Marie on mission compound

Saturday 26 October
Exploring Tartagal

Surviving railway signal, Tartagal

We have had an electric fan on continuously throughout the night, and we wake up around seven o'clock, feeling relatively fresh. The plan today is to meet an Indian leader in a reservation and then have dinner with one of his friends, an anthropologist by the name of John, whose mother lived in Torquay, and maybe meet his wife as well.

The temperature is in the upper thirties Celsius, as Ed, Marie, Sylvia, and I breakfast together. I spend the early part of the morning frenetically knocking into shape some ideas around a theme for my message to Ed's church tomorrow, my first (and probably last) opportunity to preach a sermon in Argentina.

Later, when I am feeling more relaxed, with a clear idea on what I will preach about tomorrow, Ed drives us around the small town of Tartagal, which comprises a few blocks centred on a main square, in splendid isolation and a significant distance away from any other settlements. Ed explains that there are two main groups of Indians around Tartagal, the Wichi and Guarani, who have settled in distinct parts of the town, generally on the edge, in addition to other, smaller tribal encampments.

A former railway runs along one side of the town. Although it is closed, and has been for some years, it is almost intact. There is even a rusting semaphore signal standing guard, as it were, at a level crossing, cutting a stark figure. Someone walking along the road stops and says to Ed that I am in a dangerous area for taking photographs – I need to be careful! But the signal assumes an iconic significance for me, and I am captivated by it. I just have to take a photograph.

Tartagal town centre

The local economy has taken a hit in recent years, with one of the local factories in the town, which processed eucalyptus trees, having closed down. But the building is still standing after several years, like the decaying railway infrastructure.

Ed then drives us out of the town into a forested area to the west, where they have sunk several oil or natural gas wells. We cross rivers which are more accurately described as trickles. The ground is looking parched, and the temperature rises into the lower forties Celsius in the afternoon, as Ed takes us into some of the peripheral communities, with something of a 'Wild West' feel to them. I am starting to perspire a lot; climatically at least, I am well out of my comfort zone, even though everything around here fascinates me. There is almost no vehicular traffic on the tracks and roads on the edge of Tartagal.

Tomorrow is the day of the general election in Argentina. Ed says that he has to have lived in Argentina for 20 years before he is eligible to vote. Although he comments on the principal candidates who are standing for election, (whose pictures and slogans are posted on almost every building and tree in the town), it is difficult to know which way he would vote once he is able to do so; no obvious bias can be detected, at least by me.

We return back to Ed and Marie's compound around quarter past four to await the visit of one of Ed's anthropologist friends, Chris, who is an Englishman and his wife, Elena, who is a Wichi Indian. Chris is working on translating the Bible into at least one of the local Wichi dialects. He is also a keen mountaineer. They live for much of the year in a village near Salta. For the rest of the time, Chris and Elena live among the Indians in the Gran Chaco, near the Pilcomayo River.

Chris and Elena eventually make it to Ed and Marie's home, but they have been delayed by an overturned petrol tanker and the authorities deemed it was too dangerous and too hot to approach the vehicle (nothing is said about the poor driver). The main highway between Salta and the Bolivian border has therefore been closed and a diversion route put in place, hence their delay in meeting up with us. Chris invites us to visit them in the Gran Chaco, about 60 miles to the north from Tartagal, on Sunday.

Shortly after Chris and Elena leave, another Englishman, John, also an anthropologist, who works at the local university, arrives at Ed and Marie's home. In what is quite a coincidence, his mother spent the last years of her life in a nursing home in our hometown, and we visited her a couple of times, after Ed informed John that we lived nearby in the UK and John then asked if we could visit her. John therefore wants to meet us and talk a little about his mother, who we discovered to be a loveable eccentric. I don't think she remembered us from one visit to the next, but nevertheless she always received us warmly. John's wife can't make it this afternoon, but she has sent us a present – a fibrous ostrich which she has made from a local plant, which is a typical example of local craft in this area.

In the evening, we leave Ed and Marie's home, with them, and take a short drive to a restaurant situated in the main square, the Plaza de San Martin. There's a laid back, relaxed atmosphere in the restaurant, with people of all ages milling around talking to each other before sitting down for their meal, with children playing, and nobody cares. It is a vibrant and colourful scene. Looking out into the square from the restaurant, the lighting is beginning to take effect as the darkness closes in. The plinth of the San Martin statue is pink, and this is highlighted by the lights from a forest of traditional lamps. For me, the scene looks quintessentially Latin America.

We take our places at our table in the restaurant, which relatively early in the evening is fairly quiet, at least by normal standards. John is convinced that the whole place will fill up later on. And, as time passes, he is proven to be right. But we can still hear ourselves talking, which is a good thing. Ed, John, and I spend some time discussing the implications of Brexit for the UK and the wider regional and world economy; for example, will it deliver more delicious Argentinian beef for the UK? Our discussion then leads on to the concept of people feeling excluded from power and the frustration of perceived exclusion, a topic which is clearly close to John's heart.Our waiter is highly amused by my name; he keeps repeating the words "Michael Fox" as he processes my card at the end of the meal. He then takes a group photograph of us at the table – and it turns out to be the last photograph ever taken on my camera, as it then develops a fault. From now on in this holiday, my mobile phone takes over to take the necessary photographs.

At the close of the meal, John tells us he has six children, the youngest being the only girl. He tells us he has been working on Indian land rights, and recently he defended a criollo man accused of raping an Indian woman and managed to persuade the judge to acquit him. Apparently, it was a landmark trial in Argentina, which earned him some fame. You certainly sense that he is a man with a passion, who doesn't give up on causes when he believes he has right on his side.

Eating out in Tartagal – Ed, Marie, John, Sylvia and Mike

Sunday 27 October
Delving into the Gran Chaco

Cadet's Parade, Tartagal

Not only is this the day everyone in Argentina casts their vote in the General Election, but it's the day I get to preach in Argentina, which I think is quite an honour.

The church service at the only Anglican Church in Tartagal starts at 10:30 am. The church is a modern, open and airy building, and its appearance could pass for a free church in the UK. As we enter the church sanctuary, a group of a dozen or so worshippers greet Sylvia and I. It is pleasantly cool inside, but the welcome is warm. All the women and girls come over and greet both of us with a kiss. The men and the boys also greet me, no less genuinely, but they just shake hands; that's fine by me… One young lady, possibly in her early twenties called Fernanda, who possesses an engaging smile, takes special care of Sylvia, and makes sure she is sitting comfortably.

A lady by the name of Viviana leads the service and she is effusive in her welcome. As in our experience in Bogotá two weeks ago, there is a steady trickle of families and young people coming into the church during the service through the open entrance, and the congregation has more than doubled by the time it is my turn to speak. I would guess that the majority of the fellowship this morning is under the age of 30, reflecting the demographics of this young country. Ed says that one family of five kids has been largely instrumental in transforming the makeup of the congregation from a mainly older, declining church into a younger, expanding ministry.

After about thirty minutes, Viviana calls me to the front and hands over for me to preach. I manage a couple of sentences in Spanish, explaining who we are, where we are from, and how I know Ed from years back. But Ed has offered to interpret my message into Spanish, so the pressure is off for me and I can deliver my message in English. I preach on the theme of the Christian race (based on a passage in the New Testament book of Hebrews), and I draw upon the analogy of the electoral race in Argentina.

I actually find it quite relaxing to deliver a message with someone interpreting for me; it gives me more breathing space and is less frenetic, although I have to be careful to break up what I say into relatively short sections, to enable Ed to remember what I have just said and not be saturated with information overload. I am fortunate that Ed speaks both languages fluently, and there's no danger of him getting the wrong end of the stick.

Everyone is smiling and appreciative, or at least that is my interpretation of their body language! After I close and take my seat next to Sylvia, Viviana thanks me in Spanish, and Fernanda, who is sitting immediately in front of us, turns round and mouths in English the word "thankyou"; a special moment for me. I also enjoy the music, which I would describe as contemporary without being superficial. All in all, it's fair to say that I have enjoyed my involvement in a church service in Argentina.

As we come away from the service, after having said goodbye individually to almost everyone in the building, Ed says that something I said has hit the nail on the head in relation to an ongoing pastoral issue in the church, which of course I know nothing about. God moves in mysterious ways.

After an afternoon siesta, which is appropriate in temperatures in the 40s Celsius, at around four o'clock, Ed asks me if I am interested in seeing some of the Indian resettlement schemes in the Gran Chaco, near the Pilcomayo River. Can a duck swim? The two ladies decide to stay behind and catch up on some more rest.

Ed drives the two of us out of Tartagal in his heavy-duty vehicle northwards towards the Bolivian border. On the way, he points out roadside shrines to people who are believed by many to have supernatural power. One of these people is known as Gauchito Hill, a Bolivian who was a bandit. When he was eventually caught, he put a curse on the son of the police officer who captured him and the story goes that the police officer's son died pretty soon afterwards. It doesn't sound the most edifying story to base a cult around, but the memory of the guy is big in this region. Another spiritual 'star' is a virgin by the name of Urkapina, who is reputed to have powers of healing. Again, she is from Bolivia, and she apparently seems to have overtaken a local virgin by the name of La Virgen de la Peña in terms of popularity.

This is a region in which it is estimated that there are large reserves of natural gas, and we see a pipeline under construction, which will take the resource down to Buenos Aires. We drive past a huge natural gas and oil refinery constructed in the middle of nowhere. This is quite an empty part of the country, with very few settlements or signs of human habitation to be seen.

At the top of a hill, Ed stops the car, and I am invited to alight and walk a short way to maximise the view. Ahead of me, as far as the horizon, stretches the Gran Chaco; this has the appearance of a vast sea of green. The Gran Chaco can loosely be termed a 'jungle', or 'dry' forest, which extends from Argentina to Bolivia and Paraguay. This is a breath-taking view, but even at five in the afternoon it is hot, and I don't stay out of the vehicle for long. But Ed tells me the Chaco is changing. Groups of Indians, who until recently have been warring neighbours, are being relocated in an attempt to move them beyond the flood zone of the Pilcomayo River.

Apparently, one place near here, called La Paz (Spanish for peace), was so named because three warring tribes used to be continually attacking and killing one another. When these tribes were contacted by Christian missionaries a few years ago, all three tribes accepted the Christian Gospel and the fighting stopped permanently.

We leave the recently tarmacked main road at a place by the name of Santa Maria, although there are no road signs that I can see to tell any outsiders that this is the case, and we enter a network of severely rutted earthen tracks within the Chaco forest. This area is impassable by your average two-wheel drive car, but Ed's vehicle has a high clearance and can drive off-road. We are now driving through an area which regularly floods when the Pilcomayo River overflows, usually in December and January.

This mish-mash of tracks leaves me completely disorientated, and we are also out of mobile phone contact. I push to the back of my mind what would happen if our vehicle were to break down in this place. Ed, however, is pretty sure he knows exactly where he is going, and sure enough, a few turns later on the forested tracks, we enter a small clearing, and there directly ahead of us, we see Chris and Elena sitting around a small table, along with a friend from the mission whom we met yesterday and three dogs, who are also welcoming.

Behind them is their adobe dwelling, which is situated within a compact area demarcated by timber stakes. Whenever a passing goat – of which there are many – becomes over-inquisitive in relation to Chris and Elena's home, and especially any food, the dogs bark and charge it as a pack, and the offending goat moves off. I wonder whether they act in the same way with passing pigs that wander too close to Chris and Elena's home. But the overall impression is of a peaceful atmosphere of co-existence, even among the free roaming goats, pigs, chickens, and dogs.

We are invited to sit around the table and are offered drinks. Elena drinks maté tea through a straw. A Wichi lady joins us with her three children and the maté cup is passed to her; it seems to be a fluid equivalent of passing a peace pipe. In this idyllic scene, no one in the small encampment seems anything but friendly.

At half past five, Chris says that if we are going to see the Pilcomayo River in the daylight, then we ought to leave right away. After a rough ride over undulating terrain, the vehicle emerges from the forest. A line of blue appears through a gap in the vegetation. We walk across the sandy soil and behold, we see a sizeable river. It flows from the Andes across the Gran Chaco and eventually spills out into the River Paraguay. The opposite banks of the Pilcomayo are about 300 metres apart, and the river flows on either side of sizeable sandbanks, forming a long island. The water level at this time of the year is relatively low, and the river appears deceptively benign. A wading bird, possibly an egret, is the lone occupier of the interfluvial sandbank.

The opposite bank is grassy and behind these riverine meadows there are several linear groups of trees. Chris says that the furthest line of trees that we can see is within Bolivia. This is as near as I am ever going to get to see Bolivia, at least on this holiday.

The three of us are standing on a small sandy cliff edge, with the river water lapping a few feet below us. I now notice an ominous crack in the muddy sand behind us, and before long, this slab of compacted mud will sheer off from the bank and be carried downstream. This concentrates my mind to retreat a few steps onto more secure 'terra firma'. Chris says that the course of the river will alter again during the next flooding season. As we stand there, observing the river and the verdant landscape, we spend a little time watching the sun setting on this tranquil scene; this is one of the highlights for me of our entire time in the Americas.

Back at Chris and Elena's home, we are informed that the Wichi lady with the three children returned, bringing with her a mobile phone holder made from a local fibrous plant, saying that it was a gift for me. She has also left some attractive fibrous bags, and I buy one for Sylvia; I am taking a risk, but I think she will like it.

Chris and Elena live in their adobe home for around half the year. It seems to be open to anyone walking in, and it doesn't appear to be a defensible space, offering any form of security from intruders. It also looks as simple as the other structures in the immediate neighbourhood and blends in with the rest of the Indian community. But they seem very contented living here within the forest among the Indian people.

We have to tear ourselves away from this little paradise and Ed attempts to navigate our way through the forest to the main road. At one point, Ed stops the vehicle and enquires from a local person which is the best way to re-join the main road we left a few hours earlier. But he successfully manages to re-join the main road before we have time to panic.

Ed is also keen for me to see another resettlement scheme at a place called Santa Victoria, where huge revetments have been constructed to hold back the floodwaters of the Pilcomayo River. One of the difficulties the authorities have is when the river behaves itself and doesn't flood significantly for a couple of years. When this happens, some of the Indians decide it is OK to build villages on the floodplain, only to be inundated when the river floods again by an even higher level of floodwater because the escape of the water is blocked by the recently constructed revetments, thus preventing a means of escape for the floodwaters. But the land stretching towards the river seems very tempting to settle in for the Indians; this is clearly a challenging problem to solve by education and persuasion.

Another big impact in these resettlement areas is the introduction of electricity. Not only is this increasing light pollution in tranquil areas which hitherto have been completely dark at night, but noise levels increase, and there is the potential for more disturbance. There is also a real danger that the

Indian languages will be lost as living languages, in the face of the dominance of the Spanish language, especially for the younger generation. The availability of television in the last year threatens to change the lives, languages and maybe the cultures of these peoples forever.

Ed drives back to Tartagal more slowly, as many animals tend to wander over the road during the hours of darkness. We narrowly avoid hitting a pig just as we leave Santa Victoria, and fortunately we are travelling slowly.

We make it back to Ed's home in Tartagal by 10:30. The Argentinian General Election results have already been announced, which I find impressive for such a large and diverse country. The one-time president and Peronista, Kristine Kirchner, has been sworn in as the Vice-President. I hear that there has already been a run on the Argentinian peso.

Edge of Gran Chaco, north of Tartagal

Mission Compound, Pilcomayo Valley

Chris and Ed on the banks of Pilcomayo River

Monday 28 October
The Journey back to Salta

On the banks of the Pilcomayo River, looking towards Bolivia

This is another day of packing everything and making sure we haven't left any items behind, except presents. This morning, Ed and I go into the town centre and find a professional photographer. He examines my 'poorly' camera and tells me it is the lens that has stopped functioning. This, of course, is serious, and the camera is beyond repair, at least at an inexpensive price, and it can't be done here in Tartagal. So, it's my mobile phone that I will have to use as a camera from here on in. I'm not a great lover of mobile phone photography, but I guess I am going to have to get used to it for the last few days of our travels in the Americas.

We stop in Tartagal town centre and go for a walk. On our walkabout, we witness a parade of junior police cadets, both boys and girls, on a march past, and we stop and watch the action. It's 44 degrees Celsius today, and some of the kids in the parade must be of primary school age, poor things, possibly as young as six or seven. They are kitted out in full uniform, with the national flag of Argentina draped over many of them, and some are supporting additional flags on high poles. They are all stepping out with very high steps (almost goosesteps), using a lot of energy, although I guess they are used to marching in this hot weather. Some of the kids are also playing trumpets and drums, with great gusto, it must be said.

Some of the companies of kids marching past us are being 'minded' by 'sergeant major' type characters, usually big men, who are fiercely shouting instructions to these tiny tots. At first glance, it seems unfair, but it is clear that there is great passion being displayed by these little marchers, and one senses a strong feeling of patriotism on show; there is clearly great pride in displaying the Argentinian flag. Ed comments that some of the 'battalions' have travelled quite a long way to get to this march in Tartagal; even more reason for some of them to be tired from all this activity.

In the local post office, I enquire about sending post cards to the UK. The guy behind the counter is almost over-helpful, as he advises me that if I posted my cards in Buenos Aires, it would knock six weeks off the postage time. I guess we really should have posted these cards earlier; after all, we bought them all in Colombia! So, Buenos Aires it is for posting them, then.

Walking in the centre of Tartagal, let alone marching, isn't easy for someone like me brought up in temperate latitudes, and I am continually perspiring. But at least I am not marching at a brisk pace!

In the afternoon, at about three o'clock, Ed and Marie, Sylvia and I set off for Salta. We have to drive through six roadblocks, but we are waved through at each one. We experience a great sunset over the Andes to our right.

There are at least two lines of peaks that we can see, being silhouetted against the red glow. At one point, the whole effect resembles an exploding volcano. Further on, the sky takes on the appearance of a Salvador Dali painting. Its striking beauty lasts for over half an hour before the darkness sets in. Ed gets us back to our hotel in Salta by nine o'clock. It's been a long drive for him, and we persuade Ed and Marie to stay overnight in Salta before returning and to have a meal with us at our hotel.

Ed says they will stay overnight at the bishop's residence here in the city. He apparently knows the Anglican bishop and after a short phone call he has arranged for a bed for the night there. He tells us a story, that when the current bishop was a student, he felt a call to work on translating the Bible into one of the Indian languages, Wichi. He was passing through Salta and decided to call on the then bishop at his residence. The bishop opened the door and the student asked him if there were any opportunities for him to work with the Wichi Indian people and translate the Bible into their language.

The bishop invited the student in and led him into a room where a couple of ladies were sitting. The bishop then said to the student "Please tell these ladies what you just said to me on the doorstep". Apparently, these ladies were in the middle of a prayer meeting and had just finished praying for someone to come and translate the Bible into the Wichi language. It's either instantly answered prayer or an amazing coincidence.

In our hotel, we sit down to our 'last supper' with Ed and Marie before farewell hugs all round. We have had a fantastic time with them, and we have been hugely impressed by their simple lifestyle and strong identification with the local people and minority groups, including the Indian communities.

Life, however, is rarely simple. Shortly after Ed and Marie depart, we discover that Sylvia's bag is not with us, and it must therefore still be in Ed's vehicle. A helpful receptionist called Mauricio gets me the phone number of the bishop's residence in Salta. He manages to get through to someone there and leaves a message. I also discover that I have a swollen left eye, which I put down to an over–intimate mosquito.

Minutes later, we crash out for the night, exhausted.

Sun setting over the Andes, en route to Salta

Tuesday 20 October
Excursions in Buenos Aires

I wake up with a large swelling just above my left eye. At 05:45, Mauricio the receptionist rings for a paramedic. He arrives and duly gives me a cortisone injection, which does the trick. I am also given two sets of tablets, delivered by courier.

Ed and Marie then appear in the hotel reception with Sylvia's handbag. Things are definitely looking up! After saying our final, final goodbyes to Ed and Marie, we make our way into the breakfast area. One of the waitresses, Vanesa, asks where we have been over the last few days. It's nice to know we have been missed! When I say we have been to Tartagal, she replies: "You have been to hell!" It is certainly a lot cooler here in Salta, probably around 30 degrees Celsius.

Ed receives a message on his phone from a neighbour in Tartagal. Apparently, some robbers have managed to scale the wall and steal some of his possessions. Ed and Marie's response to this news is amazing. They just shrug it off, with no signs of bitterness towards the people who have just violated their home; the material things of this world clearly have no hold over them, and they will carry on with their ministry as usual.

Our taxi driver arrives to take us to the local airport to catch our flight to Buenos Aires. He takes one look at us and says: "Get out of the car!" It's our friend Anibal, of course, who drove us up to Tartagal a few days ago. Obviously, once seen, we are never forgotten. As we get into his car, I mention the Argentinian election last Sunday, and I say to him: "A new Argentina!" He sticks his thumbs down, theatrically. I ask him for his card, on the slight chance that we may ever return to this beautiful part of the world, and he happily obliges. You never know.

At Salta airport, our elder son, Nathan, sends me via WhatsApp on my mobile phone, the highlights of last Sunday's football match back in England, in which our team won. In the crowded waiting area in the airport, Sylvia tells me to turn the sound down. But at least it isn't a clip from a Boca- River match! That really would have been a high-risk strategy.

It's a clear, sunny late morning as our small plane takes off for Buenos Aires. There are clear views to be had from the plane, and to begin with we are flying over an arid landscape, including several dry riverbeds. Over the past few days, we have seen many rivers with almost no water flowing in them, in contrast to most of the rivers back in the UK, something I am in danger of taking for granted.

Soon we are flying above the Andes. Several cordilleras are separated by narrow valleys. Some of the Andean peaks protrude above the height of the clouds in their sheer beauty. The clouds resemble ocean waves crashing against the Cornish coastline, well, with a bit of imagination.

However, before too long, all we can see is clouds, white, fluffy ones, and then the captain tells everyone that the temperature in Buenos Aires is 19 degrees C, which sounds like heaven to Sylvia and I right now. Sylvia says she thinks the captain is saying: "Good morning, ladies and gentlemans. This is the captain speaking from the toilet." At this moment, I am having serious doubts about her powers of hearing and comprehension.

We fly over the Parana Delta, and on the edge of the greater Buenos Aires urban area I spot a de lux residential estate in semi-rural surrounds. It is based on a lake with several narrow tongues of land protruding into the water, allowing every house to have direct access to the waterfront. Then we fly over a golf village with some more seriously expensive real estate.

Descending over the city in the early afternoon sun, the area looks vibrant and prosperous. From this angle, the city looks at peace with itself.

Our team comprising our guide, Mariana and our driver, Christian are waiting for us at the airport, and we are soon driving away from Buenos Aires to the north, back to the delta which we have just flown over. We drive past the impressive River stadium, where Mariana says many international matches are played. It started life in 1930, and has been progressively added to, so it now forms a complete bowl accommodating 75,000 spectators. But our time is at a premium and we have to keep on going.

Apparently, we are driving on a section of the Pan-American Highway, which should take you all the way to Panama, although Mariana adds "in theory at least". Maybe this is a project for another time. But this stretch of highway is a good, two-lane dual carriageway, maybe the best road we have travelled on in Latin America so far.

Mariana is taking us to the small town of Tigre, which is situated at the edge of the Parana Delta. There is a relaxed, European feel about this place, reinforced by the mild temperature we are experiencing today. It is also the capital of rowing in Argentina and there are waterside sculling clubs which remind me of the Thames at Henley. You can also catch sea going ships, either to Buenos Aires on the River Plate or up the Parana and Paraguay Rivers to Asuncion, the capital of Paraguay, or across the River Plate to Montevideo in Uruguay. This place could be worth coming back to when we have a bit more time to explore, and all we are going to do this afternoon is scratch the surface of this fascinating area, which looks a world apart from the urban metropolis of Buenos Aires, maybe ten miles away to the south.

The Delta comprises an extensive network of channels, and it could be described as the Buenos Aires equivalent of the Norfolk Broads. We leave the car, walk over to the waterfront and board a boat. Well, it's not quite that simple for Sylvia; she has to be lowered onto the boat in her wheelchair using a metal hoist. But it works.

Our boat sets out from the quayside, and we soon pass a naval museum, exhibiting ships that were used during the Malvinas War, getting on for 40 years ago. The distributary that we are coasting along is the Lujar River, and it separates several islands from the mainland. Mariana says there are over 80 miles of waterway in the Delta area around Tigre.

We sail past several houses that are raised off the ground, or water, on stilts or piles as a defence against flooding, and the water levels here are notorious for fluctuating markedly. Many of the dwellings are individually designed and have private jetties. Some of these houses are stylish and genuinely beautiful, some are pretentious and some look like they belong to a different planet. No two houses look alike. Expensive real estate abounds, both terrestrial and floating. But it's a verdant and varied environment, which holds my attention for long periods, and some of the houses blend in well with their natural and artificial landscaping. Herons and other wading birds abound in this almost surreal environment.

We pass one impressive waterside house, dating from 1855, with a more recent huge glass case constructed (circa 1990). It is called the House of Sarmiento, named after one of Argentina's most respected politicians of the nineteenth century, whom I think actually lived here at one time, and Mariana says it is now a fine art museum as well as a memorial to the great man, with mature landscaping in its grounds. Another interesting but perhaps unsurprising feature is that all the kids on the Delta go to school by water bus; I wonder if the novelty ever wears off. Mariana thinks that people from all social classes reside in the Delta, but I'm not so sure, even though some of the more eccentric looking structures seem on the verge of collapse.

There aren't too many people on our boat, and we occupy the raised stern, as Sylvia's wheelchair can't go onto the lower deck (at least not without being physically lowered by several people). This is fine for us, and we have this relatively secluded area all to ourselves, where we take advantage of a gentle breeze and great views of the waterway and all the fascinating houses lining the waterfront. Would I like to live in one of these dwellings? I'm not sure; I would probably consider this to be too remote a location, and in all likelihood, I couldn't afford to live in this riverine paradise anyway.

Mariana is quite happy to talk about a wide range of subjects, and we have the undisturbed opportunity to do so on the boat. We touch on many subjects, including Argentine politics, and the record of the outgoing president and his administration. His biggest problem seems to be failing to keep a lid on inflation, which has plagued this country for such a long time. Also, he wasn't that charismatic a speaker, and that seems to have counted heavily against him.

Apparently in the recent election last Sunday, Buenos Aires voted against the trend of the rest of the country and found itself on the losing side. One of Mariana's sayings, which amuses me, is that the Peronists love the poor so much that they want to multiply them! Mariana's English is pretty good, but she uses the word "fluvial" quite a lot, rather than, say, riverside. I say to her that back in the UK, the only people who would use this word regularly, or even at all, are geologists!

Once we are back on dry land, we have a late lunch at the - I'm not making this up – Estacion Fluvial (Riverside Station). So, this is where Mariana gets the word from! I think the temperature, in the late afternoon, has risen above 19 degrees C. But maybe it's the effect of coming off the breezy boat onto dry land.

Sylvia and Mariana go off to spend my money on presents, leaving me to savour the atmosphere of the restaurant and surrounding shopping area. Christian our driver is given orders to go and buy stamps for my post cards showing scenes of Colombia. The restaurant seems to be frequented by the local fashionistas, with their tight-fitting apparel, bright colours and arrogant strides, but it makes for good theatre.

Once we have eaten, our tour continues through some interesting little towns. San Fernando is a yachting centre, and we drive through its pleasant, tree-lined streets. The place has a very settled feel to it. A great place to go dog walking, me thinks.

We stop at the neighbouring settlement of San Isidro, which Mariana says dates from the 1850s. It has elegant buildings and parks and seems to me to be an Argentine version of London's Kensington. By the 1880s, wealthy families from Buenos Aires were snapping up these properties as second homes, probably spurred on by the (then) newly constructed railway giving direct access to the city centre. This peaceful and delightful oasis of relative calm, seemingly a thousand miles away from the big city, has several cobbled streets and orange trees.

The neo-Gothic San Isidro Cathedral displays a superb, slender, and elegant steeple and faces a small park, beyond which is the commuter railway which still has a regular service into the heart of Buenos Aires. The cathedral is too beautiful to miss, and Mariana and I step inside and pause for a few minutes. Just outside, the Plaza Mitre has a statue of a former president by the same name, who presided over this nation in the nineteenth century.

Christian, our driver, takes us back along the coast road into the city of Buenos Aires, past extensive housing schemes, which look more substantial than the favelas of Rio and Bogotá. There is something 'higgledy-piggledy' about them, and they appear to be built on top of each other. But if they are meeting a desperate housing need, then who am I to question them? Mariana says they are low-cost schemes funded by the Government.

Looking down from a bridge, we catch a superb view of the main railway station in the city, the Estacion Retiro, dominating the view with its huge and magnificent two-spanned train shed. It's almost worth a return trip to this place, to take some photographs of the station structure, the expansive track layout, and hopefully a couple of the blue trains.

Christian turns into Calle Maipu and parks opposite the Hotel Pulitzer, where we are welcomed back by the reception staff. After dumping our cases, we cross the street to a pizza place, where neither of us can finish the generous portions we have been served and finish with a chocolate ice cream, which is naughty but nice.

Back in our hotel, I turn on the TV and watch a football programme. In one of the games shown, and it's of a lower league match, the cameras keep focusing on an old man seated on a chair by the touch line. One team score four times in about ten minutes, and each time the ball hits the back of the net, the jubilant players all run over to this old man and hug and kiss him. Who is this old man that the TV cameras keep on showing?

Then the penny drops – it's the great Maradonna! This is the man who once said that one of his goals against England in a world cup game was scored by the "hand of God". As every Englishman knows, the goal was scored by the hand of Maradonna! The referee in that game was clearly not a theologian, and he never spotted the infringement. But hand of God or not, he's had a good night tonight with his new team.

After a full day, we are in bed around midnight.

Parana Delta near Tigre, north of Buenos Aires

Wednesday 30 October
Farewell to Latin America

Our breakfast area seems to have been taken over by a lively group of German ladies of a certain age. One of the party goes up to the lady at the serving bar, says something very loud to her in German, sticks two fingers in the air (presumably to indicate the amount), points in one direction and asks "Jah?". The lady at the serving bar points in the same direction, nods and all seems to be well.

After our breakfast, I take our cases from our bedroom to the lift, en route to checking out of the hotel. When the lift stops at our floor, a German lady stands inside it. She remains in the lift and says something in German, which Sylvia would have understood but she's still in our bedroom. The German lady continues to stand in the stationary lift. After what seems a long time with neither of us going anywhere, I eventually squeeze past her with my two cases, and at the last minute before the lift moves, she walks out onto the landing. But the lift then ignores my pressing for the ground floor and takes me up to the fourth floor! I reprogram it to go down to the ground floor hotel reception. At the first floor, where I was several minutes ago, in walks the same German lady, presses for the basement – and then gets out at level 2! At the third attempt I make it to the ground floor reception with our cases intact.

After checking out of the hotel, we still have some time before Mariana and Christian are due to collect us and take us to the airport for our flight to London. It's a beautiful, clear morning and we take a stroll around the block. We find a pharmacist where Sylvia buys a packet of throat sweets and some cream to smear around her mouth. We have just succeeded in getting through to our doctor and dentist back in the UK, and we have arranged for Sylvia to see her doctor on Friday. In fact, there's quite a list of things to do, having been away for a month.

Just as we return to the hotel, we spot Christian and Mariana, who tell us they got here five minutes early, and we transfer our cases to their car. Once we are on the move, Mariana asks me to complete a customer satisfaction survey. I tell her I can dictate it for her to tap into her phone, as it would take me as far as Uruguay to complete it as a text message on her phone. I say out loud: "The guide was terrible; the driver was dangerous!" Fortunately, they both laugh, and I haven't upset them. In fact, I say very kind things about both of them, and I feel that we have been a great team over the tours around Buenos Aires that we have had the privilege to go on. We have had a great time with them, getting to know this beautiful city.

Mariana accompanies us into the airport departure lounge, where we say our goodbyes. She has been a great guide and we have got on really well together. I feel Mariana has become a friend, and she has already sent us a selfie of the three of us when we were on the boat in the Delta yesterday. You never know, she may bring her family over to visit us in the UK someday.

Our British Airways direct flight to London Heathrow departs a few minutes early in the early afternoon. Our flight is smooth, on the whole, and we are immersed in cloud cover for almost the entire route, shutting out any views of land or sea.

The guy sitting next to me on the plane somehow manages to get last night's English football results off his laptop, and I learn that by some miracle, Manchester United have achieved the feat of winning three games in a row, which is almost a collector's item these days.

House of Sarmiento, Parana Delta

Thursday 31 October
A Long Homecoming

As usual, I don't sleep on the plane, but the BA stewards are superb, and make the thirteen-and-a-half-hour flight pass as comfortably as possible. We touch down at London Heathrow airport early in the morning in pleasant, cool weather.

The Great Western Railway staff at London's Paddington Station are also really helpful, and I think it's fair to say that Sylvia's only disappointment is that the train she spots with the name 'Paddington Bear' inscribed on it turns out not to be our train back to the West Country.

Eating out in Bogotá – Ingrid, Sylvia, Natalie, Gabriel, and Mike

www.ingramcontent.com/pod-product-compliance
Lightning Source LLC
LaVergne TN
LVHW020413070526
838199LV00054B/3594